SIEM Systems: Design and Deployment

James Relington

DEDICATION

To those who seek knowledge, inspiration, and new perspectives—
may this book be a companion on your journey, a spark for curiosity,
and a reminder that every page turned is a step toward discovery.

AKNOWLEDGEMENTS

I would like to express my deepest gratitude to everyone who contributed to the creation of this book. To my colleagues and mentors, your insights and expertise have been invaluable. A special thank you to my family and friends for their unwavering support and encouragement throughout this journey.

Introduction to SIEM Systems

Security Information and Event Management (SIEM) systems have become an essential part of modern cybersecurity infrastructures. As organizations face an ever-increasing number of cyber threats, SIEM solutions provide the ability to collect, analyze, and respond to security events in real time. These systems are designed to aggregate data from multiple sources, correlate events, and detect anomalies that may indicate malicious activity. By centralizing security event data and offering advanced analytics, SIEM systems enable organizations to strengthen their security posture and comply with regulatory requirements.

The concept of SIEM evolved from two earlier technologies: Security Information Management (SIM) and Security Event Management

(SEM). SIM systems were primarily focused on the long-term storage and analysis of security logs, while SEM solutions provided real-time event correlation and alerting. The integration of these two capabilities resulted in SIEM, a more comprehensive approach to security monitoring. SIEM solutions help security teams detect potential threats before they escalate into full-scale breaches. With the increasing complexity of IT environments and the rise of sophisticated cyberattacks, organizations rely on SIEM to gain visibility into their networks and respond to incidents more effectively.

SIEM systems function by collecting logs from various sources, including firewalls, intrusion detection systems, antivirus software, operating systems, and cloud environments. These logs are then normalized and correlated to identify patterns that may indicate suspicious activity. The ability to analyze data from diverse sources allows SIEM platforms to provide context-aware security alerts. Without a centralized logging and monitoring system, organizations would struggle to detect coordinated attacks that leverage multiple attack vectors. SIEM solutions provide a unified view of security events, enabling security analysts to detect complex threats that might otherwise go unnoticed.

One of the most valuable aspects of SIEM is its ability to support compliance initiatives. Many industries are subject to strict regulations that require organizations to monitor and retain security logs. Regulations such as GDPR, HIPAA, PCI DSS, and SOX mandate that companies implement logging and auditing mechanisms to track access to sensitive data and detect unauthorized activities. SIEM solutions simplify compliance reporting by automating log collection, retention, and analysis. Organizations can generate detailed reports to demonstrate their adherence to security policies and regulatory requirements. This capability not only helps businesses avoid costly fines but also enhances their overall security posture.

As cyber threats evolve, SIEM technology continues to advance. Traditional SIEM solutions relied heavily on rule-based detection methods, which required security teams to define correlation rules manually. While these rules are effective for detecting known threats, they struggle to identify emerging attack techniques. To address this limitation, modern SIEM platforms incorporate artificial intelligence and machine learning capabilities. These advanced analytics enable SIEM systems to detect previously unknown threats by identifying deviations from normal behavior. Behavioral analysis, anomaly detection, and user entity behavior analytics (UEBA) are becoming integral components of next-generation SIEM solutions.

Despite their benefits, SIEM systems also present several challenges. One of the most common issues organizations face is the high volume of alerts generated by SIEM platforms. Without proper tuning, SIEM systems can overwhelm security teams with false positives, making it difficult to prioritize real threats. Configuring a SIEM solution to reduce noise while maintaining a high detection rate requires careful fine-tuning of correlation rules and thresholds. Additionally, SIEM implementation can be complex and resource-intensive. Organizations must invest in skilled personnel who can manage, maintain, and optimize their SIEM systems effectively. The cost of deployment, including licensing fees, infrastructure requirements, and ongoing maintenance, can also be a barrier for small and medium-sized enterprises.

The increasing adoption of cloud services has introduced new challenges and opportunities for SIEM technology. Traditional SIEM solutions were designed for on-premises environments, but as businesses migrate to cloud-based infrastructures, SIEM vendors have developed cloud-native solutions. Cloud SIEM platforms offer greater scalability and flexibility, allowing organizations to monitor cloud workloads, SaaS applications, and hybrid environments. These modern SIEM solutions leverage big data technologies to process massive amounts of security event data efficiently. Additionally, cloud-based SIEM systems reduce the burden of managing infrastructure, as they are maintained by service providers who handle updates and optimizations.

Integration with other security tools is another critical aspect of SIEM systems. To maximize effectiveness, SIEM platforms must work seamlessly with endpoint detection and response (EDR) solutions, threat intelligence feeds, vulnerability management tools, and security orchestration, automation, and response (SOAR) platforms. By integrating with these technologies, SIEM enhances an organization's ability to detect, investigate, and respond to security incidents in a timely manner. The use of threat intelligence feeds allows SIEM systems to correlate internal security events with known indicators of compromise, improving detection accuracy.

As cyber threats continue to evolve, organizations must continuously improve their SIEM implementations. Regular updates, rule tuning, and integration with emerging security technologies are necessary to ensure that SIEM solutions remain effective. Security teams must also invest in training to keep up with the latest threats and best practices for managing SIEM systems. A well-implemented SIEM solution is a crucial asset for any organization, providing the visibility and intelligence needed to protect against cyberattacks and ensure regulatory compliance.

The Evolution of SIEM Technology

The development of Security Information and Event Management (SIEM) technology has been a gradual process shaped by the ever-growing complexity of cyber threats and the increasing need for advanced security solutions. Over the years, SIEM has evolved from basic log management tools to sophisticated platforms that leverage artificial intelligence, machine learning, and cloud-native architectures to detect and respond to security incidents in real time. This evolution has been driven by the rapid expansion of digital infrastructures, the rise of regulatory compliance requirements, and the growing sophistication of cyber adversaries who continue to find new ways to bypass traditional security controls.

Early SIEM systems emerged from the need to consolidate security event data across multiple systems. Before SIEM, organizations relied on individual security tools such as firewalls, intrusion detection systems, and antivirus software to monitor and protect their environments. However, these tools operated in silos, making it difficult for security teams to correlate events and identify patterns indicative of a coordinated attack. In response to this challenge, Security Information Management (SIM) and Security Event Management (SEM) technologies were developed to address different aspects of security monitoring.

SIM solutions focused primarily on log storage, analysis, and compliance reporting. These systems allowed organizations to collect logs from various devices and retain them for extended periods to meet regulatory requirements. While useful for forensic investigations, SIM solutions lacked real-time monitoring capabilities, making them ineffective for detecting active threats as they occurred. On the other hand, SEM solutions were designed to analyze security events in real time, providing alerts when suspicious activity was detected. However, SEM tools often struggled with scalability, as they were limited by the computing power required to process vast amounts of event data.

As organizations recognized the limitations of SIM and SEM as standalone solutions, the concept of SIEM emerged as a unified approach that combined the strengths of both technologies. Early SIEM platforms provided centralized log management and real-time event correlation, enabling security teams to detect and respond to threats more efficiently. These early systems relied heavily on rule-based correlation engines, where analysts defined specific conditions that would trigger alerts. While this approach was effective for detecting known attack patterns, it required constant rule updates to keep up with evolving threats.

The increasing complexity of IT environments and the rapid growth of cyber threats exposed several challenges in early SIEM implementations. One of the most significant issues was the high volume of alerts generated by SIEM systems, leading to alert fatigue among security analysts. Many organizations found that their SIEM solutions produced an overwhelming number of false positives, making it difficult to distinguish between legitimate threats and routine network activity. Additionally, SIEM systems required significant manual effort to configure and maintain, which created operational burdens for security teams.

To address these challenges, SIEM vendors began incorporating more advanced analytics and automation features into their platforms. The introduction of machine learning and artificial intelligence revolutionized SIEM technology by enabling systems to detect anomalies without relying solely on predefined rules. Instead of requiring security teams to manually create correlation rules, machine learning algorithms could analyze vast amounts of security data to identify unusual behavior patterns that might indicate an attack. This shift significantly improved the accuracy of threat detection while reducing false positives.

The rise of cloud computing and distributed IT infrastructures further transformed SIEM technology. Traditional on-premises SIEM solutions struggled to scale effectively in environments where workloads were distributed across multiple data centers and cloud platforms. As organizations adopted hybrid and multi-cloud architectures, SIEM vendors developed cloud-native solutions capable of ingesting security data from a wide range of sources, including cloud applications, containers, and serverless environments. These modern SIEM platforms leveraged big data technologies to process massive amounts of log data efficiently, enabling real-time analysis and faster response times.

Another significant advancement in SIEM technology was the integration of Security Orchestration, Automation, and Response (SOAR) capabilities. SOAR solutions extended SIEM functionality by automating response actions based on predefined workflows. Instead of merely generating alerts, SIEM systems equipped with SOAR capabilities could automatically trigger incident response procedures, such as isolating compromised endpoints, blocking malicious IP addresses, or notifying security teams of critical threats. This automation helped organizations reduce their mean time to respond (MTTR) and improved their overall security posture.

The role of threat intelligence in SIEM also became increasingly important as cyber threats grew more sophisticated. Traditional SIEM systems relied primarily on internal log data, but modern SIEM platforms integrated external threat intelligence feeds to enhance their detection capabilities. By correlating security events with known indicators of compromise (IOCs) from threat intelligence sources, SIEM systems became more effective at identifying and mitigating advanced persistent threats (APTs) and zero-day attacks. This integration allowed security teams to stay ahead of emerging threats by leveraging real-time intelligence from global cybersecurity communities.

As the cybersecurity landscape continues to evolve, SIEM technology is expected to undergo further advancements. The increasing use of artificial intelligence, behavioral analytics, and predictive modeling will enhance the ability of SIEM systems to anticipate threats before they materialize. Additionally, as organizations embrace Zero Trust security models, SIEM platforms will play a crucial role in enforcing access controls and monitoring user behavior across networks. The convergence of SIEM with extended detection and response (XDR) solutions will further improve threat visibility by integrating endpoint, network, and cloud security data into a unified platform.

Despite the continuous evolution of SIEM, challenges remain. Organizations must ensure that their SIEM deployments are properly tuned to minimize alert fatigue and optimize detection capabilities. Skilled personnel are required to manage and interpret SIEM-generated alerts effectively, highlighting the need for ongoing cybersecurity training and workforce development. Furthermore, as attackers develop new techniques to evade detection, SIEM vendors must continuously innovate to keep pace with the evolving threat landscape.

The journey of SIEM technology from basic log management to advanced, AI-driven threat detection reflects the broader evolution of cybersecurity itself. As businesses become more reliant on digital infrastructures, the need for effective security monitoring and incident response solutions will only grow. The continued refinement and expansion of SIEM capabilities will remain a cornerstone of modern cybersecurity strategies, ensuring that organizations can detect, analyze, and mitigate threats in an increasingly complex digital world.

Understanding Security Event Management (SEM)

Security Event Management (SEM) is a crucial component of modern cybersecurity strategies, designed to provide real-time monitoring, event correlation, and alerting mechanisms for organizations seeking to detect and respond to security incidents. SEM systems are built to analyze security events as they occur, enabling security teams to identify threats quickly and mitigate potential risks before they escalate. The primary function of SEM is to collect, process, and correlate event data from various sources within an IT environment, allowing organizations to gain immediate visibility into security incidents that could compromise their systems.

The foundation of SEM lies in its ability to aggregate logs and event data from diverse security tools, including firewalls, intrusion detection and prevention systems (IDS/IPS), endpoint protection platforms, authentication services, and network monitoring solutions. By centralizing event data, SEM eliminates information silos and provides a holistic view of an organization's security posture. This centralized approach ensures that security teams are not limited by isolated alerts from individual security tools but can instead analyze patterns across multiple sources to detect coordinated attacks.

One of the core capabilities of SEM is event correlation, which involves analyzing log data to identify meaningful connections between seemingly unrelated security events. Traditional security tools often generate massive amounts of alerts, many of which may appear benign when viewed in isolation. However, when correlated with other events, certain activities may reveal a broader security threat. For example, a single failed login attempt on an administrative account may not raise concerns, but multiple failed login attempts followed by a successful authentication from an unusual geographic location could indicate a compromised account. SEM systems use predefined correlation rules and analytics to connect these events and generate high-fidelity alerts for security analysts.

The ability to provide real-time analysis and alerting is another fundamental aspect of SEM. Unlike Security Information Management (SIM) solutions, which focus on long-term log storage and compliance reporting, SEM operates in near real-time to detect ongoing threats. This capability is essential in modern cybersecurity, where attackers continuously exploit vulnerabilities and attempt to gain unauthorized access to critical assets. SEM platforms process incoming event data continuously, applying correlation rules and predefined security policies to identify potential threats as they emerge. When a suspicious activity is detected, SEM generates an alert, enabling security teams to investigate and take immediate action.

To enhance threat detection accuracy, SEM solutions often incorporate threat intelligence feeds that provide real-time information on known malicious actors, suspicious IP addresses, and emerging attack techniques. By integrating external threat intelligence with internal event data, SEM systems improve their ability to recognize and mitigate advanced persistent threats (APTs), zero-day exploits, and targeted attacks. This integration enables security teams to correlate internal security incidents with global threat trends, allowing them to stay ahead of evolving threats and take proactive measures to protect their systems.

Another critical feature of SEM is the ability to automate responses to detected security incidents. While traditional SEM solutions primarily focused on alerting security teams, modern implementations now include automated response mechanisms to mitigate threats before they cause significant damage. For instance, if SEM detects an ongoing brute-force attack against a privileged user account, it can trigger an automated response to temporarily lock the account, block the source IP address, or escalate the incident to a higher-priority security workflow. These automated responses reduce the mean time to detect (MTTD) and mean time to respond (MTTR), significantly improving an organization's overall security posture.

One of the challenges associated with SEM implementation is the potential for alert fatigue, where security analysts become overwhelmed by the sheer volume of alerts generated by the system. Improperly tuned SEM solutions can produce excessive false positives, leading to inefficiencies and wasted resources. To address this issue, organizations must carefully fine-tune their correlation rules, implement noise reduction techniques, and utilize machine learning-based anomaly detection to prioritize alerts based on severity and relevance. Advanced SEM solutions incorporate behavioral analytics to distinguish between normal user activity and potential threats, further improving the accuracy of alerts.

Scalability is another important consideration when deploying SEM. As organizations expand their IT infrastructure, the volume of security events generated by endpoints, cloud services, and network devices increases exponentially. A well-designed SEM system must be capable of handling large amounts of event data while maintaining real-time processing capabilities. Many modern SEM solutions leverage cloud-based architectures and big data technologies to ensure scalability without compromising performance. By utilizing distributed processing models and optimized data indexing, cloud-based SEM platforms can efficiently process and analyze massive log datasets from geographically dispersed environments.

The evolution of cyber threats has also influenced the role of SEM in security operations. Traditional rule-based correlation models, while effective in detecting known attack patterns, struggle to identify sophisticated threats that do not match predefined rules. To address this limitation, modern SEM platforms integrate machine learning and artificial intelligence-driven analytics to identify anomalies and detect novel attack techniques. By analyzing historical data and recognizing deviations from established behavioral baselines, SEM systems can detect subtle indicators of compromise that might otherwise go unnoticed. This adaptive approach enhances an organization's ability to identify and respond to emerging threats in real time.

Integration with other security solutions is essential for maximizing the effectiveness of SEM. Organizations often deploy SEM alongside Security Orchestration, Automation, and Response (SOAR) platforms, Endpoint Detection and Response (EDR) tools, and cloud security solutions to create a comprehensive security ecosystem. The ability to share threat intelligence, automate incident response workflows, and integrate with forensic analysis tools strengthens an organization's ability to defend against cyber threats. When SEM is used in conjunction with SIEM, it forms a powerful security monitoring framework that combines real-time event correlation with long-term log analysis and compliance reporting.

As cybersecurity threats continue to evolve, the importance of SEM in security operations cannot be overstated. Organizations must continually refine their SEM implementations by updating correlation rules, integrating new data sources, and leveraging advanced analytics to detect threats with greater accuracy. Security teams must also ensure that they have the necessary expertise and resources to effectively manage and respond to SEM-generated alerts. A properly implemented SEM solution provides organizations with the visibility and intelligence needed to detect and mitigate threats in real time, reducing the risk of security breaches and data compromise.

Understanding Security Information Management (SIM)

Security Information Management (SIM) is a foundational element of modern cybersecurity strategies, providing organizations with the ability to collect, store, analyze, and manage security-related data from various sources. Unlike Security Event Management (SEM), which focuses on real-time monitoring and threat detection, SIM is designed primarily for log management, forensic analysis, and compliance reporting. By centralizing and retaining security logs, SIM enables organizations to maintain a comprehensive record of network activities, helping security teams investigate past incidents, identify trends, and ensure adherence to regulatory requirements.

The primary function of SIM systems is to aggregate logs from multiple devices and applications across an organization's IT infrastructure. Firewalls, intrusion detection and prevention systems (IDS/IPS), antivirus software, authentication servers, cloud environments, and endpoint protection platforms generate vast amounts of security logs daily. These logs contain valuable information about system access, user activity, network traffic, and potential security incidents. Without a centralized system to collect and organize this data, organizations would struggle to track security events across their networks. SIM platforms provide a structured approach to log management, allowing security teams to access historical records quickly and efficiently.

Long-term log storage is one of the key capabilities of SIM solutions. Many regulatory frameworks, such as the General Data Protection Regulation (GDPR), the Health Insurance Portability and Accountability Act (HIPAA), the Payment Card Industry Data Security Standard (PCI DSS), and the Sarbanes-Oxley Act (SOX), require organizations to retain security logs for extended periods. Compliance with these regulations is essential for avoiding fines and legal penalties. SIM solutions ensure that security logs are stored securely, indexed for easy retrieval, and protected against unauthorized access. By maintaining an archive of security events, organizations can demonstrate compliance with industry standards and provide audit trails for regulatory inspections.

Forensic investigation is another critical use case for SIM. When a security incident occurs, organizations must be able to trace its origins, determine the extent of the damage, and identify the attacker's methods. SIM platforms enable security analysts to conduct post-incident investigations by querying historical log data and reconstructing the sequence of events leading up to the breach. By analyzing past security events, organizations can uncover hidden vulnerabilities, detect patterns indicative of malicious activity, and refine their security policies to prevent future attacks. The ability to conduct in-depth forensic analysis is particularly valuable in cases of insider threats, advanced persistent threats (APTs), and targeted cyberattacks, where attackers attempt to remain undetected for extended periods.

Threat intelligence integration enhances the capabilities of SIM by correlating historical log data with known indicators of compromise (IOCs). By comparing security logs against external threat intelligence feeds, SIM solutions can identify connections between past events and emerging threats. This approach helps organizations uncover hidden attack patterns that may have been overlooked at the time of the incident. Advanced SIM platforms incorporate machine learning and behavioral analytics to identify anomalies in historical data, allowing security teams to recognize suspicious activities that deviate from normal operational baselines. These insights enable organizations to strengthen their security defenses by proactively addressing potential risks before they escalate into full-scale attacks.

Log normalization and categorization play a crucial role in the effectiveness of SIM systems. Different security devices and applications generate logs in varying formats, making it challenging to analyze data consistently. SIM platforms normalize these logs into a standardized format, ensuring that security teams can interpret and correlate information across multiple sources. By categorizing logs based on severity, source, and event type, SIM systems make it easier to identify critical security incidents and prioritize investigation efforts. Without proper log normalization, organizations would face difficulties in correlating data from diverse security tools, reducing their ability to detect meaningful security trends.

Scalability is an important consideration when implementing SIM solutions. As organizations expand their IT environments, the volume of security logs grows exponentially. Traditional on-premises SIM solutions often struggle to handle the increasing data loads generated by modern cloud-based infrastructures, IoT devices, and remote work environments. To address this challenge, cloud-based SIM solutions have emerged, offering greater scalability, flexibility, and processing power. These modern SIM platforms leverage distributed storage, big data analytics, and artificial intelligence to process and analyze vast amounts of log data efficiently. Cloud-based SIM solutions also reduce the burden of infrastructure management, as vendors handle system updates, maintenance, and optimization.

The integration of SIM with Security Information and Event Management (SIEM) platforms has further enhanced its capabilities. While SIM focuses on long-term log management, SIEM combines SIM with real-time event correlation and security monitoring. This convergence allows organizations to benefit from both historical log analysis and proactive threat detection. By integrating SIM with SIEM, security teams gain a comprehensive security intelligence platform that enables continuous monitoring, compliance reporting, and advanced threat analysis. The ability to access both real-time and historical security data improves an organization's ability to detect and respond to security incidents effectively.

Despite its many advantages, SIM presents certain challenges. One of the primary concerns is the storage and management of vast amounts of log data. Retaining logs for extended periods requires significant storage capacity and efficient data indexing to ensure quick retrieval when needed. Organizations must also implement strict access controls and encryption mechanisms to protect sensitive security logs from unauthorized access. Another challenge is ensuring that logs are collected from all relevant sources, as gaps in log collection can create blind spots in security analysis. Regular audits and log validation processes help ensure that SIM systems capture and retain the necessary security data.

Maintaining an effective SIM implementation requires ongoing refinement and adaptation to evolving security threats. Organizations must regularly update their log correlation rules, fine-tune data retention policies, and integrate new data sources to maintain visibility across their environments. Security teams must also receive training in forensic analysis techniques to maximize the value of historical log data in threat investigations. As cyber threats continue to grow in sophistication, organizations must leverage SIM capabilities to gain deeper insights into security trends, improve incident response strategies, and enhance their overall cybersecurity posture.

The role of SIM in modern security operations continues to expand as organizations recognize the importance of comprehensive log management and historical security analysis. With advancements in machine learning, cloud computing, and automation, SIM solutions are becoming more intelligent and efficient, enabling organizations to process and analyze security data at unprecedented scales. By leveraging SIM as part of a broader cybersecurity strategy, organizations can improve their ability to detect, investigate, and prevent security threats, ensuring the protection of critical assets and sensitive data in an increasingly complex digital landscape.

Core Components of a SIEM System

A Security Information and Event Management (SIEM) system is a powerful tool designed to enhance an organization's security posture by collecting, analyzing, and correlating security event data from multiple sources. By centralizing security logs and providing real-time insights, SIEM systems enable security teams to detect threats, investigate incidents, and maintain regulatory compliance. The functionality of a SIEM system is built upon several core components, each of which plays a critical role in ensuring its effectiveness. These components work together to provide organizations with comprehensive security monitoring and incident response capabilities, making SIEM an essential component of modern cybersecurity infrastructures.

The log collection and aggregation component serves as the foundation of any SIEM system. This component is responsible for gathering logs from various security devices, applications, and network infrastructure, including firewalls, intrusion detection and prevention systems, antivirus software, operating systems, cloud platforms, and databases. Logs contain valuable information about user activities, authentication attempts, system changes, network traffic, and potential security threats. By aggregating logs into a centralized repository, SIEM systems eliminate data silos and enable security teams to analyze security events in a unified manner. Effective log collection ensures that no critical events go unnoticed and provides the data necessary for correlation and analysis.

Log normalization and parsing are essential for transforming raw log data into a standardized format that can be effectively analyzed. Different security tools generate logs in various formats, making it challenging to interpret and correlate events across multiple sources. The normalization process converts these logs into a uniform structure, ensuring consistency and enabling efficient search and analysis. Parsing mechanisms extract relevant information from log entries, categorizing them based on event types, severity levels, timestamps, and sources. Without proper normalization and parsing, security teams would struggle to identify meaningful patterns within vast amounts of log data, reducing the overall effectiveness of the SIEM system.

Event correlation is one of the most critical components of SIEM, allowing security teams to identify relationships between seemingly unrelated security events. Attackers often employ sophisticated tactics that involve multiple stages, such as reconnaissance, credential theft, privilege escalation, and lateral movement. When viewed in isolation, individual security events may not appear malicious, but when correlated with other events, they can reveal coordinated attack patterns. SIEM correlation engines use predefined rules, machine learning algorithms, and behavioral analytics to detect anomalies and generate alerts when suspicious activity is identified. This capability enables organizations to recognize and respond to threats before they result in data breaches or system compromises.

Real-time alerting and notification mechanisms enable security teams to respond swiftly to potential security incidents. When a SIEM system detects an anomaly or matches an event against a predefined correlation rule, it generates an alert to notify security analysts. These alerts can be prioritized based on severity, ensuring that critical threats receive immediate attention. SIEM platforms often integrate with Security Orchestration, Automation, and Response (SOAR) solutions to automate responses to security events, reducing the time required to contain threats. Automated alerts can trigger predefined workflows, such as blocking an IP address, disabling a compromised user account, or initiating an investigation into suspicious activities.

Security dashboards and reporting capabilities provide visibility into an organization's security posture by presenting SIEM-generated data in an intuitive and digestible format. Dashboards allow security analysts to monitor key security metrics, track active threats, and review historical trends. Customizable reporting features enable organizations to generate compliance reports for regulatory frameworks such as GDPR, HIPAA, PCI DSS, and SOX. These reports help organizations demonstrate their adherence to security policies and identify areas that require improvement. Advanced visualization techniques, such as heat maps and trend graphs, further enhance the ability to interpret security data and make informed decisions.

User and entity behavior analytics (UEBA) is a modern enhancement to SIEM systems that improves threat detection by analyzing normal user behavior and identifying deviations that may indicate malicious activity. Traditional SIEM systems rely heavily on predefined rules and correlation patterns, but attackers are constantly evolving their tactics to bypass rule-based detections. UEBA employs machine learning and statistical models to establish baselines of typical behavior for users, devices, and applications. When an entity exhibits behavior that deviates significantly from its baseline, such as accessing sensitive data at unusual hours or making multiple failed login attempts from different locations, the SIEM system generates an alert. By incorporating UEBA, SIEM solutions enhance their ability to detect insider threats, compromised accounts, and advanced persistent threats.

Threat intelligence integration enhances the capabilities of a SIEM system by providing real-time insights into known cyber threats. SIEM platforms ingest threat intelligence feeds containing information about malicious domains, IP addresses, file hashes, and attacker tactics. By correlating internal security events with external threat intelligence, SIEM systems improve their ability to identify and block threats before they cause harm. Threat intelligence helps organizations stay ahead of emerging threats by leveraging data from global threat-sharing communities, security research teams, and government agencies. The integration of SIEM with threat intelligence feeds strengthens an organization's ability to detect and respond to cyber threats in an increasingly complex threat landscape.

Data retention and storage play a vital role in enabling forensic investigations and compliance auditing. Many security incidents are not immediately detected, requiring organizations to review historical logs to uncover attack footprints. SIEM systems must efficiently store and manage large volumes of security logs, ensuring that data remains accessible for extended periods. Advanced indexing techniques allow security analysts to perform rapid searches across historical logs to investigate incidents and identify root causes. Regulatory requirements often mandate that logs be retained for months or even years, making storage management a crucial consideration for SIEM deployments. Cloud-based SIEM solutions offer scalable storage options, reducing the burden of maintaining on-premises infrastructure for log retention.

Integration with other security solutions enhances the overall effectiveness of a SIEM system by enabling seamless communication between different security tools. SIEM platforms work best when they integrate with Endpoint Detection and Response (EDR) solutions, vulnerability management tools, identity and access management (IAM) systems, and network security appliances. This interoperability ensures that security teams have a holistic view of their organization's security posture and can respond to threats more effectively. The ability to ingest data from various sources and correlate it within the SIEM environment strengthens an organization's ability to detect sophisticated cyberattacks and coordinate response efforts across multiple security domains.

A well-implemented SIEM system is more than just a log management tool; it is a critical component of an organization's security infrastructure. By leveraging log collection, event correlation, real-time alerting, behavior analytics, and threat intelligence integration, SIEM platforms provide a comprehensive security monitoring and incident response framework. As cyber threats continue to evolve, SIEM systems must adapt by incorporating advanced technologies such as artificial intelligence, machine learning, and automation to stay ahead of attackers. Organizations that invest in optimizing their SIEM capabilities gain a strategic advantage in detecting, analyzing, and mitigating security threats, ensuring the protection of their digital assets and sensitive data.

The Role of SIEM in Modern Cybersecurity

Security Information and Event Management (SIEM) has become a cornerstone of modern cybersecurity, providing organizations with the ability to detect, analyze, and respond to security incidents in real time. As cyber threats continue to evolve in complexity and sophistication, organizations require advanced solutions to maintain visibility across their networks and ensure proactive threat mitigation. SIEM plays a critical role in enhancing security operations by aggregating and correlating vast amounts of data from various sources, helping security teams identify anomalies and take immediate action. By centralizing security monitoring and response capabilities, SIEM enables organizations to strengthen their defenses against cyberattacks and ensure compliance with industry regulations.

One of the most significant contributions of SIEM to modern cybersecurity is its ability to collect and analyze security logs from multiple sources. Organizations operate complex IT environments that include on-premises systems, cloud platforms, mobile devices, Internet of Things (IoT) endpoints, and remote workstations. Each of these components generates security logs that contain valuable insights into user activity, system access, network traffic, and potential threats. Without a centralized system to manage these logs, security teams would struggle to detect patterns indicative of cyber threats. SIEM consolidates this information into a single platform, normalizing the data and making it searchable, which allows analysts to quickly identify security incidents that require investigation.

Event correlation is another fundamental function of SIEM that enhances its role in cybersecurity. Attackers often employ multi-stage attack strategies that involve reconnaissance, exploitation, privilege escalation, and data exfiltration. If these events are analyzed in isolation, they may not trigger any security alarms. SIEM correlates these events across different data sources to identify potential threats that might otherwise go unnoticed. By applying correlation rules, SIEM systems can recognize when multiple seemingly benign activities form part of a larger attack campaign. This capability is essential for detecting advanced persistent threats (APTs), insider threats, and sophisticated cyberattacks that evade traditional security controls.

Real-time threat detection and alerting capabilities make SIEM a valuable asset for security operations centers (SOCs). Cyber threats evolve at an unprecedented rate, with attackers constantly devising new techniques to bypass security defenses. SIEM systems continuously monitor security events, applying predefined correlation rules and behavioral analytics to detect anomalies that may indicate malicious activity. When an unusual or suspicious event is detected, SIEM generates alerts that notify security teams of potential threats. These alerts allow security analysts to investigate incidents before they escalate, reducing the risk of data breaches, financial losses, and reputational damage.

The role of SIEM extends beyond threat detection to include automated incident response. Modern SIEM solutions integrate with Security Orchestration, Automation, and Response (SOAR) platforms to streamline response efforts and reduce manual intervention. When a security incident occurs, SIEM can automatically trigger predefined response actions, such as isolating compromised devices, blocking malicious IP addresses, disabling suspicious user accounts, or escalating incidents to security analysts. By automating these processes, organizations can significantly reduce the time it takes to contain threats, minimizing the impact of cyberattacks and improving overall security resilience.

Compliance with regulatory requirements is another area where SIEM plays a crucial role in modern cybersecurity. Organizations across various industries must adhere to strict security and privacy regulations, such as the General Data Protection Regulation (GDPR), the Health Insurance Portability and Accountability Act (HIPAA), the Payment Card Industry Data Security Standard (PCI DSS), and the Sarbanes-Oxley Act (SOX). These regulations mandate the implementation of robust security monitoring and auditing mechanisms to protect sensitive data and ensure accountability. SIEM simplifies compliance efforts by automating log collection, retention, and reporting. Organizations can generate detailed compliance reports that demonstrate adherence to security policies and regulatory requirements, reducing the risk of fines and legal consequences.

SIEM enhances cybersecurity by integrating with threat intelligence feeds that provide real-time information on emerging threats, known attack signatures, and malicious actors. By correlating internal security events with external threat intelligence, SIEM can identify indicators of compromise (IOCs) and detect threats that align with known attack patterns. Threat intelligence integration enables organizations to stay ahead of cyber adversaries by proactively blocking threats before they infiltrate their networks. This capability is particularly valuable in combating zero-day exploits, ransomware campaigns, and nation-state-sponsored attacks that continuously evolve to evade detection.

As organizations migrate to cloud-based infrastructures, SIEM has adapted to support cloud security monitoring. Traditional SIEM solutions were designed for on-premises environments, but modern deployments must accommodate hybrid and multi-cloud architectures. Cloud-native SIEM solutions provide organizations with visibility into cloud workloads, containers, serverless applications, and SaaS platforms. These solutions leverage big data analytics and scalable architectures to process massive amounts of security logs efficiently. Cloud-based SIEM platforms reduce the burden of infrastructure management by offering managed security services that handle system updates, threat intelligence integration, and performance optimization.

Behavioral analytics and machine learning have further expanded the capabilities of SIEM by enabling more accurate threat detection. Traditional SIEM systems relied heavily on rule-based detections, which required security teams to define correlation rules manually. While effective for identifying known threats, rule-based detections struggle to detect novel attack techniques that deviate from established patterns. Modern SIEM solutions incorporate machine learning algorithms that analyze historical data to establish behavioral baselines for users, devices, and applications. When a deviation from normal behavior is detected, SIEM generates alerts that indicate potential security risks. This approach improves threat detection accuracy and reduces false positives, allowing security teams to focus on genuine threats.

The integration of SIEM with endpoint detection and response (EDR), network security tools, and identity and access management (IAM) solutions strengthens its role in modern cybersecurity. Organizations require a holistic security strategy that provides end-to-end visibility across their digital assets. SIEM acts as a central security hub, aggregating data from various security tools and providing contextual insights into security incidents. By correlating endpoint activity, network traffic, and user authentication logs, SIEM helps organizations detect lateral movement, privilege abuse, and other attack techniques used by cybercriminals. This comprehensive approach enhances threat hunting capabilities and supports proactive security measures.

As cyber threats continue to evolve, SIEM must adapt to keep pace with emerging attack methodologies. Organizations must continuously refine their SIEM deployments by updating correlation rules, integrating new data sources, and leveraging advanced analytics to improve threat detection capabilities. Security teams must also invest in ongoing training to ensure they can effectively interpret SIEM-generated alerts and respond to security incidents. By leveraging the full capabilities of SIEM, organizations can enhance their security operations, reduce risk exposure, and protect critical assets in an increasingly digital and interconnected world.

SIEM vs. Other Security Solutions

Security Information and Event Management (SIEM) is often compared to other security solutions that play critical roles in protecting an organization's IT infrastructure. While SIEM provides centralized security monitoring, event correlation, and compliance reporting, other security technologies focus on specific aspects of cybersecurity, such as endpoint protection, network security, and threat detection. Understanding the differences between SIEM and other security solutions is essential for organizations looking to build a comprehensive security strategy that leverages the strengths of each tool while minimizing gaps in threat detection and response.

One of the key distinctions between SIEM and traditional security tools is its ability to aggregate and analyze security events from multiple sources. Unlike standalone security solutions that operate independently, SIEM integrates logs and events from firewalls, intrusion detection and prevention systems (IDS/IPS), antivirus software, cloud services, identity management platforms, and endpoint security tools. This centralization allows security teams to correlate seemingly unrelated events and detect coordinated attacks that might otherwise go unnoticed. Without SIEM, organizations would have to manually analyze data from multiple security solutions, increasing the likelihood of missing critical threats.

Intrusion detection and prevention systems (IDS/IPS) are often seen as alternatives to SIEM, but they serve different functions. IDS monitors network traffic for suspicious activity and generates alerts when anomalies are detected. IPS takes this a step further by actively blocking malicious traffic in real time. While IDS/IPS solutions provide valuable network security capabilities, they do not offer the centralized log management, correlation, and historical analysis provided by SIEM. An IDS might detect a network intrusion attempt, but without SIEM, security teams would not have the broader context needed to determine whether the attempt was part of a larger attack campaign involving compromised credentials or lateral movement within the network.

Endpoint Detection and Response (EDR) solutions focus on monitoring individual devices, such as workstations, servers, and mobile devices, for signs of compromise. EDR tools collect detailed telemetry from endpoints, detecting threats such as malware infections, unauthorized access attempts, and suspicious process executions. Unlike SIEM, which aggregates logs from various sources, EDR solutions specialize in endpoint-level visibility and response. While EDR can detect and contain threats at the endpoint level, it lacks the ability to correlate security events across an entire IT environment. SIEM complements EDR by ingesting endpoint telemetry and correlating it with network, cloud, and identity-related events to provide a more comprehensive threat detection framework.

Network security solutions, such as firewalls and secure web gateways (SWG), are designed to control and monitor network traffic to prevent unauthorized access and malicious activity. Firewalls enforce access control policies by blocking or allowing traffic based on predefined rules, while secure web gateways filter web traffic to protect users from accessing malicious websites. While these solutions are critical for enforcing perimeter security, they do not provide the analytical and forensic capabilities of SIEM. A firewall may block an attempted intrusion, but without SIEM, security teams would lack the ability to investigate whether the attacker attempted multiple entry points or whether the same threat actor targeted other systems within the organization.

Threat intelligence platforms (TIPs) provide organizations with up-to-date information on emerging cyber threats, attack techniques, and known indicators of compromise (IOCs). These platforms collect intelligence from global sources, enabling security teams to proactively defend against new threats. While SIEM solutions often integrate with threat intelligence feeds, they serve different purposes. SIEM focuses on correlating internal security events to detect anomalies, while TIPs provide external threat context to enhance detection and response efforts. When integrated with SIEM, threat intelligence enhances an organization's ability to detect attacks that align with known adversary tactics and techniques.

Security Orchestration, Automation, and Response (SOAR) platforms extend the capabilities of SIEM by automating security workflows and response actions. While SIEM detects and alerts on security incidents, SOAR platforms help security teams respond more efficiently by automating repetitive tasks such as blocking malicious IP addresses, quarantining compromised endpoints, and notifying relevant personnel. Without SIEM, SOAR platforms would lack the event correlation and threat detection capabilities needed to initiate automated responses. The combination of SIEM and SOAR creates a more efficient security operations workflow, reducing the time required to contain and mitigate threats.

Identity and Access Management (IAM) solutions focus on controlling and monitoring user access to systems, applications, and data. IAM solutions enforce authentication policies, manage user privileges, and detect unauthorized access attempts. While IAM provides critical access control mechanisms, it does not offer the real-time monitoring and event correlation capabilities of SIEM. A compromised user account might be detected by an IAM system, but without SIEM, security teams would not have the ability to correlate the compromised account's activities with other suspicious events, such as failed login attempts from foreign locations or access to sensitive files outside of normal business hours. SIEM enhances IAM by providing behavioral analytics that detect anomalies in user behavior, helping organizations identify potential insider threats and account takeovers.

Cloud security solutions, such as Cloud Access Security Brokers (CASBs) and Cloud Security Posture Management (CSPM) tools, are designed to protect cloud-based environments from misconfigurations, unauthorized access, and data breaches. CASBs provide visibility into cloud application usage, enforce security policies, and detect data exfiltration attempts. CSPM tools continuously monitor cloud configurations to ensure compliance with security best practices. While these tools provide valuable cloud security capabilities, they do not offer the centralized event correlation that SIEM provides. A CASB might detect an unusual data transfer from a cloud storage account, but without SIEM, security teams would lack the ability to correlate that event with other suspicious activities, such as a phishing attempt targeting an employee or an unauthorized login from a foreign IP address.

Organizations often deploy multiple security solutions to cover different aspects of cybersecurity, but SIEM serves as the glue that brings them together into a unified security framework. SIEM does not replace IDS/IPS, EDR, firewalls, TIPs, SOAR, IAM, or cloud security tools; rather, it enhances their effectiveness by aggregating, correlating, and analyzing data from all these sources. Without SIEM, security teams would be forced to rely on isolated security tools, leading to fragmented visibility and inefficient threat detection. By integrating these tools into a SIEM platform, organizations gain a holistic view of their security posture, enabling faster threat detection, streamlined investigations, and more effective incident response.

As cyber threats become more sophisticated, organizations must move beyond traditional security tools and adopt a layered security strategy that includes SIEM as a central component. By leveraging SIEM alongside complementary security solutions, organizations can improve their ability to detect, analyze, and mitigate cyber threats in real time. The ability to correlate data across endpoints, networks, cloud environments, and user identities provides security teams with a comprehensive understanding of their threat landscape. SIEM acts as the backbone of modern security operations, ensuring that security teams have the intelligence and insights needed to protect their digital assets from an ever-evolving array of cyber threats.

Key Features of an Effective SIEM System

An effective Security Information and Event Management (SIEM) system is a critical component of modern cybersecurity operations, providing organizations with the ability to detect threats, analyze security events, and respond to incidents in a timely manner. SIEM solutions have evolved significantly over the years, incorporating advanced technologies such as machine learning, behavioral analytics, and cloud-based architectures to enhance their capabilities. A well-designed SIEM system must integrate seamlessly with an organization's existing security infrastructure, enabling security teams to monitor, investigate, and mitigate potential risks efficiently. The effectiveness of a SIEM system is determined by its ability to aggregate security data, correlate events, generate accurate alerts, automate responses, and support compliance requirements.

Log collection and aggregation form the foundation of an effective SIEM system. Organizations generate vast amounts of security logs from firewalls, intrusion detection systems, endpoint protection platforms, cloud environments, authentication services, and network devices. Without a centralized mechanism to collect and store these logs, security teams would struggle to gain visibility into potential threats. An effective SIEM solution must be capable of ingesting logs from diverse sources in real time, ensuring that all security-related events are captured for analysis. The ability to process structured and unstructured log data is essential for providing a comprehensive view of an organization's security posture.

Normalization and parsing are essential capabilities that allow SIEM systems to standardize and categorize log data from multiple sources. Different security tools generate logs in various formats, making it challenging to correlate events without a consistent structure. SIEM solutions must normalize logs into a unified format, enabling analysts to search, filter, and analyze security events efficiently. Parsing mechanisms extract relevant metadata from raw logs, such as timestamps, IP addresses, user activity, and event severity. Proper normalization and parsing ensure that SIEM-generated alerts are accurate and meaningful, reducing the likelihood of false positives and enabling faster threat detection.

Event correlation is one of the most powerful features of an effective SIEM system. Cyber attackers often employ multi-stage attack strategies that involve lateral movement, privilege escalation, and data exfiltration. Individual security events may appear harmless when analyzed in isolation, but when correlated with other related events, they may reveal signs of an ongoing attack. SIEM solutions use predefined correlation rules, machine learning algorithms, and behavioral analytics to identify patterns that indicate potential security threats. The ability to correlate events from multiple data sources enhances an organization's ability to detect advanced persistent threats (APTs) and coordinated cyberattacks.

Real-time threat detection and alerting capabilities are critical for enabling rapid incident response. Security teams rely on SIEM-generated alerts to identify potential security incidents and take immediate action. An effective SIEM system must support customizable alerting mechanisms, allowing organizations to prioritize threats based on severity, impact, and risk level. Modern SIEM platforms incorporate risk-based alerting, which assigns a threat score to each security event, helping analysts focus on the most critical incidents. By reducing noise and filtering out low-priority alerts, SIEM solutions prevent alert fatigue and ensure that security teams can respond efficiently to genuine threats.

User and Entity Behavior Analytics (UEBA) has become an essential feature of modern SIEM solutions, enabling more accurate threat detection through behavioral analysis. Traditional rule-based detection methods struggle to identify emerging threats that do not match predefined attack patterns. UEBA enhances SIEM capabilities by establishing behavioral baselines for users, endpoints, and applications. When an entity exhibits activity that deviates significantly from its historical behavior, the SIEM system generates an alert for further investigation. This approach is particularly effective for detecting insider threats, compromised accounts, and unauthorized access attempts that might otherwise go unnoticed.

Threat intelligence integration enhances SIEM's ability to detect known cyber threats and improve response times. An effective SIEM system must incorporate external threat intelligence feeds that provide real-time updates on malicious domains, IP addresses, file hashes, and attacker tactics. By correlating internal security events with global threat intelligence, SIEM solutions can identify and block threats before they cause damage. Organizations that leverage threat intelligence within their SIEM environment gain proactive defense capabilities, allowing them to stay ahead of emerging cyber threats and respond to attacks more effectively.

Automated response and remediation capabilities are essential for reducing the time required to contain and mitigate security incidents. Modern SIEM systems integrate with Security Orchestration, Automation, and Response (SOAR) platforms to automate threat response workflows. When a security event meets predefined criteria, the SIEM system can trigger automated actions such as blocking an IP address, disabling a compromised user account, or isolating an infected endpoint. By automating routine security tasks, SIEM solutions help security teams focus on higher-priority investigations while minimizing the impact of cyber threats.

Scalability and performance optimization are crucial factors that determine the effectiveness of a SIEM deployment. Organizations generate an increasing volume of security data as they expand their IT environments, adopt cloud-based infrastructures, and deploy IoT devices. A robust SIEM system must be capable of handling large-scale data ingestion, processing, and analysis without performance degradation. Cloud-native SIEM solutions leverage big data technologies and distributed architectures to provide scalable security monitoring, enabling organizations to analyze millions of security events per second. Performance optimization ensures that SIEM systems can provide real-time threat detection and analysis without introducing delays or bottlenecks.

Compliance reporting and audit capabilities are critical for organizations that must adhere to regulatory requirements such as GDPR, HIPAA, PCI DSS, and SOX. An effective SIEM system simplifies compliance efforts by automating log retention, generating audit reports, and providing real-time visibility into security controls. Security teams can use SIEM-generated compliance reports to demonstrate adherence to industry regulations, conduct internal audits, and identify areas for improvement. By maintaining a centralized record of security events, organizations can meet legal obligations while improving their overall security posture.

Integration with other security tools enhances the overall effectiveness of SIEM by enabling seamless data sharing and threat detection across multiple platforms. Organizations deploy various security solutions, including Endpoint Detection and Response (EDR), Identity and Access Management (IAM), Intrusion Detection Systems (IDS), and Cloud Security Posture Management (CSPM). A well-designed SIEM system must integrate with these tools to provide a unified security monitoring framework. The ability to correlate security data from multiple sources improves threat visibility, strengthens forensic investigations, and enables more effective incident response.

Advanced analytics and artificial intelligence (AI) are transforming SIEM capabilities, enabling more intelligent threat detection and predictive analysis. Traditional SIEM solutions relied on static rule-based detections, which required frequent manual updates to remain effective. AI-powered SIEM platforms leverage machine learning algorithms to detect unknown threats, analyze historical attack trends, and predict potential security risks. By continuously adapting to evolving attack techniques, AI-driven SIEM systems improve detection accuracy, reduce false positives, and enhance security teams' ability to respond to emerging threats.

A highly effective SIEM system combines multiple features to provide comprehensive security monitoring, threat detection, and incident response capabilities. Organizations that invest in optimizing their SIEM deployments benefit from improved visibility into security events, faster threat mitigation, and stronger compliance management. As cyber threats become more sophisticated, SIEM solutions must evolve to incorporate advanced analytics, automation, and cloud-based scalability. Security teams must continuously refine their SIEM configurations, update correlation rules, and integrate new data sources to maximize their system's effectiveness in protecting digital assets from cyber threats.

Log Collection and Normalization

Log collection and normalization are fundamental processes within a Security Information and Event Management (SIEM) system, enabling organizations to consolidate security data from diverse sources and transform it into a structured format for analysis. Every IT infrastructure generates an immense volume of logs from various security devices, applications, servers, and network components. These logs contain valuable insights into system activity, authentication events, access attempts, and potential security threats. However, raw logs are often inconsistent in format, making it challenging for security teams to extract meaningful insights. By collecting and normalizing logs, SIEM solutions create a unified data structure that allows for efficient correlation, threat detection, and compliance reporting.

Effective log collection is essential for maintaining visibility across an organization's IT environment. Security devices such as firewalls, intrusion detection systems (IDS), antivirus software, and endpoint protection platforms generate logs that provide real-time information about security events. Network devices, including routers, switches, and proxies, produce logs related to traffic patterns, connectivity, and access control policies. Cloud platforms and virtualized environments generate logs detailing API calls, user authentication, and resource utilization. In addition to security-related logs, operating systems and business applications produce activity logs that track user interactions, system modifications, and software execution. Collecting logs from all these sources ensures that no critical security event goes undetected, allowing security analysts to monitor potential threats comprehensively.

The process of log collection typically involves agents, APIs, and network-based data collection methods. Many SIEM solutions deploy lightweight software agents on endpoints and servers to collect log data in real time. These agents transmit logs to a centralized SIEM platform, ensuring that security teams receive up-to-date information.

In cloud-based environments, SIEM solutions often rely on API integrations to pull logs from cloud service providers, security tools, and SaaS applications. Network-based collection methods, such as Syslog and NetFlow, allow SIEM systems to gather logs from network devices without requiring direct agent installations. By using a combination of these techniques, organizations can aggregate security logs efficiently while minimizing the impact on system performance.

Log normalization is a crucial step in preparing raw log data for analysis. Different security tools and devices generate logs in various formats, with inconsistent structures, field names, and data representations. Without normalization, security analysts would struggle to correlate logs from different sources, making it difficult to detect coordinated cyberattacks. Normalization converts raw logs into a standardized format by extracting key attributes such as timestamps, source IP addresses, destination IP addresses, user identities, event types, and severity levels. By enforcing a uniform log format, SIEM systems enable efficient searching, filtering, and correlation of security events.

Timestamp normalization is one of the most important aspects of the log normalization process. Logs generated by different systems often use different time formats and time zones, which can create inconsistencies when analyzing security events. If a SIEM system does not normalize timestamps correctly, security analysts may encounter difficulties in reconstructing the sequence of events during an investigation. Normalization ensures that all timestamps are converted to a standard format, typically using Coordinated Universal Time (UTC), allowing for accurate event correlation and forensic analysis across multiple log sources.

Event categorization is another essential component of log normalization. Security logs can represent a wide range of activities, including authentication attempts, file access events, network connections, malware detections, and system modifications. Categorizing events based on their type and severity helps security teams prioritize threats and focus on high-risk activities. Many SIEM platforms use predefined event taxonomies, such as the Common Event Format (CEF) or the Open Security Event Metadata (OSEM) framework, to classify log data into standardized categories. This categorization enables security analysts to filter logs based on specific event types and conduct targeted investigations more effectively.

The normalization process also involves mapping different field names to a standardized schema. Various security devices may refer to the same data attribute using different terminology. For example, a firewall log might use the field name "src_ip" to represent a source IP address, while an intrusion detection system might use "source_address" for the same data. Without normalization, these differences would make it difficult to correlate related events across multiple log sources. SIEM systems resolve this issue by mapping disparate field names to a common schema, ensuring that all logs adhere to a consistent structure.

Normalization enhances the efficiency of security analytics and event correlation. When logs are structured in a uniform format, SIEM systems can apply advanced analytics techniques to identify anomalies and detect patterns indicative of cyber threats. Normalized logs allow for the creation of correlation rules that link multiple related events into a single security incident. For example, a failed login attempt followed by a successful authentication from a suspicious IP address may indicate a compromised account. By normalizing log data, SIEM systems improve the accuracy of threat detection and reduce the number of false positives that security teams must investigate.

Log enrichment further enhances the value of collected and normalized logs by adding contextual information that helps analysts understand security events more clearly. Enrichment involves augmenting raw log data with additional details, such as threat intelligence indicators, geolocation data, and user identity information. Threat intelligence feeds can provide real-time updates on known malicious IP addresses, domains, and file hashes, allowing SIEM systems to flag suspicious activities. Geolocation data can help identify unusual access patterns, such as login attempts from foreign countries that deviate from a user's normal behavior. User identity enrichment can correlate log data with identity and access management (IAM) systems to determine whether an account involved in a security event has elevated privileges or past security violations.

Retaining and managing normalized log data is also a critical consideration for organizations using SIEM systems. Many regulatory frameworks, such as GDPR, HIPAA, PCI DSS, and SOX, require organizations to store security logs for extended periods to support audit and compliance efforts. SIEM solutions must implement efficient data storage and indexing mechanisms to ensure that historical log data remains accessible for forensic investigations and compliance reporting. Advanced SIEM platforms leverage big data technologies and cloud-based storage solutions to manage large volumes of normalized log data efficiently while optimizing query performance for rapid searches.

The combination of effective log collection and normalization provides organizations with a powerful foundation for security monitoring, threat detection, and incident response. Without proper log management, security teams would struggle to piece together security incidents, identify attack patterns, and comply with regulatory requirements. By centralizing log collection and applying normalization techniques, SIEM systems enhance an organization's ability to analyze security events in real time, detect sophisticated cyber threats, and maintain a proactive security posture. As cyber threats continue to evolve, the importance of accurate and comprehensive log management will remain a cornerstone of modern security operations.

Event Correlation Techniques

Event correlation is one of the most critical functions of a Security Information and Event Management (SIEM) system, allowing organizations to detect complex attack patterns and security incidents that would otherwise go unnoticed. Cyberattacks are often executed in multiple stages, involving different tactics and techniques that span various parts of an organization's IT infrastructure. If security events are analyzed in isolation, detecting a sophisticated attack becomes extremely difficult. Event correlation techniques enable SIEM systems to link seemingly unrelated security events across different data sources, revealing suspicious activities and providing security teams with a more comprehensive view of potential threats. By leveraging advanced event correlation mechanisms, organizations can significantly improve their threat detection capabilities and respond to incidents more effectively.

Pattern matching is one of the most widely used event correlation techniques in SIEM systems. This approach involves defining specific correlation rules that identify predefined attack patterns or suspicious behaviors. When security events match the conditions set by these rules, the SIEM system generates an alert for further investigation. For example, if a SIEM system detects multiple failed login attempts on a privileged account followed by a successful authentication from an unusual IP address, it may trigger an alert indicating a potential brute-force attack or account compromise. Pattern matching is effective for detecting known attack techniques, but it requires continuous updates to correlation rules as attackers develop new evasion methods.

Rule-based correlation expands on pattern matching by allowing security teams to define conditional logic that links multiple security events together. Instead of treating events as isolated occurrences, rule-based correlation creates relationships between different log entries to identify potential security incidents. This technique enables organizations to detect multi-stage attacks, such as phishing campaigns that lead to credential theft and subsequent unauthorized access. For example, a rule may be configured to detect an email containing a suspicious link, followed by a login attempt from an unusual location, and then an attempt to access sensitive data. By correlating these events, the SIEM system can determine that an attacker may have successfully compromised an account and is attempting to escalate privileges.

Time-based correlation is another essential technique used in SIEM platforms to detect security threats that unfold over a specific timeframe. Many cyberattacks involve a sequence of events that occur within a defined time window. If these events happen too far apart, they may not be related, but when they occur in quick succession, they may indicate a coordinated attack. SIEM systems apply time-based correlation by monitoring event sequences and establishing relationships between events that happen within a set duration. For example, if a system registers multiple failed login attempts followed by a successful login from a new device within a short period, the SIEM system can flag it as a possible credential-stuffing attack.

Statistical correlation techniques use mathematical models and data analysis to detect deviations from normal activity. Instead of relying solely on predefined rules, statistical correlation examines historical log data to establish baseline behaviors for users, applications, and network activity. When an event significantly deviates from the expected pattern, the SIEM system generates an alert. This approach is particularly useful for detecting insider threats and advanced persistent threats (APTs), where attackers attempt to remain undetected by avoiding known attack patterns. By leveraging statistical analysis, SIEM systems can detect anomalies such as an employee accessing sensitive files at unusual hours or a system suddenly generating an abnormally high volume of network traffic.

Machine learning-based correlation enhances SIEM capabilities by using artificial intelligence to identify complex attack patterns that traditional rule-based methods might miss. Machine learning models analyze vast amounts of security data to uncover hidden relationships between events and predict potential threats. These models continuously learn from historical data, refining their detection capabilities over time. By using clustering algorithms and classification techniques, machine learning can distinguish between normal user behavior and potentially malicious activities. This approach significantly reduces the number of false positives, enabling security teams to focus on high-priority threats rather than being overwhelmed by irrelevant alerts.

Behavioral correlation techniques focus on detecting changes in user and entity behavior that may indicate security risks. Instead of analyzing security events in isolation, SIEM systems equipped with User and Entity Behavior Analytics (UEBA) correlate activities across multiple data sources to identify behavioral anomalies. If an employee who typically logs in from a corporate office suddenly begins accessing systems from multiple locations in different countries within a short timeframe, behavioral correlation can flag this as suspicious. Similarly, if an administrator account that normally performs routine maintenance tasks starts executing privilege escalation commands, the SIEM system can generate an alert for further investigation.

Threat intelligence-based correlation enhances SIEM detection capabilities by integrating real-time threat intelligence feeds into event correlation processes. By comparing internal security events with external threat intelligence data, SIEM systems can identify indicators of compromise (IOCs) such as known malicious IP addresses, domains, and file hashes. If an organization detects an outbound connection to an IP address associated with a known threat actor, threat intelligence-based correlation can link that event to other suspicious activities, such as unauthorized data transfers or lateral movement attempts. This approach enables organizations to proactively defend against emerging threats by leveraging up-to-date intelligence from cybersecurity research teams and global threat-sharing networks.

Multi-source correlation techniques take event correlation a step further by combining security events from different layers of an organization's IT infrastructure. Cyberattacks often involve multiple attack vectors, including network breaches, endpoint compromises, and cloud-based exploits. SIEM systems that implement multi-source correlation analyze security events across different environments to detect complex attack campaigns. For example, if a network firewall detects an attempted intrusion, an endpoint security tool detects malware installation, and a cloud security solution identifies unauthorized access, multi-source correlation can connect these events to reveal a coordinated attack. This holistic approach provides security teams with greater context, enabling them to respond to threats more effectively.

Automated response correlation integrates SIEM event correlation with Security Orchestration, Automation, and Response (SOAR) platforms to take immediate action against detected threats. When a SIEM system correlates security events and identifies a high-risk incident, automated response correlation can trigger predefined workflows to contain the threat. For example, if the SIEM system detects an unauthorized login followed by an attempt to access critical systems, it can automatically revoke the compromised user's credentials, isolate affected endpoints, and notify security teams. By automating incident response actions, organizations can significantly reduce the time required to mitigate security risks and prevent further damage.

Event correlation techniques continue to evolve as cyber threats become more sophisticated. Organizations must continuously refine their SIEM correlation rules, incorporate advanced analytics, and integrate new data sources to enhance threat detection capabilities. By combining traditional rule-based approaches with machine learning, behavioral analytics, and threat intelligence, SIEM systems provide security teams with a powerful tool for identifying and mitigating cyber threats in real time. As attackers develop new evasion techniques, the ability to correlate security events across different systems and detect complex attack patterns remains a critical component of modern cybersecurity strategies.

Real-Time Security Monitoring

Real-time security monitoring is a critical function of a Security Information and Event Management (SIEM) system, enabling organizations to detect, analyze, and respond to security threats as they occur. Cyberattacks are becoming more sophisticated, and attackers often exploit vulnerabilities within minutes of discovering them. Without real-time monitoring, organizations may not detect threats until significant damage has already occurred, leading to data breaches, financial losses, and reputational harm. SIEM solutions provide continuous monitoring capabilities by aggregating security events from multiple sources, analyzing patterns in real time, and alerting security teams to potential threats before they escalate.

One of the fundamental aspects of real-time security monitoring is continuous log collection from various security devices, applications, and IT infrastructure components. Organizations generate massive amounts of security event data from firewalls, intrusion detection and prevention systems (IDS/IPS), endpoint protection platforms, authentication servers, cloud environments, and business applications. Each of these sources produces logs that contain valuable information about system activity, user access, network traffic, and potential security incidents. SIEM systems collect these logs in real time, ensuring that security analysts have immediate visibility into suspicious activities across the entire organization.

To effectively process and analyze the large volume of security events generated every second, SIEM systems use advanced event correlation techniques. Attackers often use multiple stages to infiltrate a network, escalate privileges, and exfiltrate data. Individually, these actions may appear harmless, but when correlated with other security events, they may indicate a serious attack. Real-time correlation enables SIEM systems to link seemingly unrelated events across multiple sources and detect patterns indicative of cyber threats. For example, a system might detect a failed login attempt followed by a successful login from an unfamiliar IP address and then an attempt to access sensitive files. By correlating these events in real time, the SIEM system can trigger an alert and prompt security analysts to investigate.

Threat intelligence integration enhances real-time security monitoring by providing contextual information about known cyber threats. SIEM solutions often integrate with external threat intelligence feeds that provide up-to-date data on malicious IP addresses, domains, file hashes, and attack tactics. When a SIEM system detects network traffic to a known malicious domain or an authentication attempt from a suspicious IP address, it can cross-reference the event with threat intelligence databases and issue an alert. This proactive approach helps organizations detect emerging threats before they cause harm. Threat intelligence-based monitoring also improves the accuracy of SIEM alerts by reducing false positives and focusing on high-risk activities.

User and entity behavior analytics (UEBA) plays a crucial role in real-time security monitoring by identifying deviations from normal behavior patterns. Traditional SIEM systems rely on predefined rules to detect threats, but attackers often develop new tactics that do not match known attack signatures. UEBA enhances SIEM capabilities by analyzing user activities, establishing behavioral baselines, and detecting anomalies that may indicate insider threats, compromised accounts, or unauthorized access attempts. If a user who typically logs in from a corporate office suddenly attempts to access systems from multiple locations around the world within a short period, the SIEM system can flag this as suspicious behavior and trigger an alert. By continuously monitoring behavioral patterns, organizations can detect and mitigate threats that traditional rule-based methods might miss.

Automated response mechanisms are becoming increasingly important in real-time security monitoring, reducing the time it takes to contain and neutralize security threats. When a SIEM system detects an active attack, it can trigger automated workflows to respond immediately. Integration with Security Orchestration, Automation, and Response (SOAR) platforms enables SIEM solutions to execute predefined actions, such as blocking malicious IP addresses, isolating compromised endpoints, revoking user privileges, or notifying security teams. Automated responses help organizations mitigate threats more quickly, minimizing the potential impact of cyberattacks and preventing attackers from gaining a foothold within the network.

Real-time security monitoring also involves anomaly detection techniques that identify unusual system activities based on historical data analysis. Many organizations have complex IT environments with thousands of users, devices, and applications generating security events. By analyzing historical data, SIEM systems can determine what constitutes normal behavior and detect deviations that may indicate a security breach. Anomaly detection algorithms use machine learning models to analyze factors such as login frequency, access patterns, data transfer volumes, and network activity levels. If an endpoint suddenly starts communicating with an external server at an unusual rate or a database experiences a spike in unauthorized queries, the SIEM system can generate an alert for further investigation.

Dashboards and visualization tools play a key role in real-time security monitoring by providing security teams with an intuitive interface to track ongoing threats and security trends. SIEM dashboards display real-time data on key security metrics, such as failed login attempts, network traffic anomalies, and malware detections. Security analysts can customize dashboards to focus on specific areas of concern, such as cloud security, privileged user activity, or network intrusion attempts. Visualization tools, such as heat maps and threat maps, provide graphical representations of attack sources, affected systems, and high-risk activities, allowing security teams to quickly assess the threat landscape and prioritize their response efforts.

Scalability is a crucial factor in real-time security monitoring, as organizations generate increasing amounts of security data from cloud environments, remote workforces, and IoT devices. Traditional SIEM solutions often struggle to process large volumes of log data in real time, leading to delays in threat detection. Cloud-based SIEM solutions leverage big data analytics and distributed processing to handle massive amounts of security event data efficiently. By using scalable cloud architectures, organizations can ensure that their SIEM systems maintain real-time monitoring capabilities, even as their IT environments grow in complexity.

Incident response workflows are an integral part of real-time security monitoring, enabling organizations to act quickly when a security event occurs. A well-designed SIEM system provides predefined response playbooks that guide security teams through the process of investigating, containing, and mitigating threats. When an alert is triggered, security analysts can follow standardized procedures to assess the severity of the incident, gather relevant log data, and determine the appropriate course of action. Automated response workflows further enhance incident response by executing immediate remediation actions, such as quarantining infected devices, blocking unauthorized access attempts, and revoking compromised credentials.

The ability to integrate with other security tools enhances the effectiveness of real-time security monitoring. SIEM systems work best when they interconnect with Endpoint Detection and Response (EDR) platforms, Identity and Access Management (IAM) solutions, firewall logs, and cloud security controls. This integration ensures that security teams have a holistic view of their organization's security posture, allowing them to detect and respond to threats across multiple attack vectors. By consolidating security data from different sources, SIEM platforms improve situational awareness and reduce blind spots in threat detection.

Continuous tuning and optimization are necessary to ensure that real-time security monitoring remains effective. Organizations must regularly update correlation rules, refine alerting thresholds, and incorporate new threat intelligence sources to improve detection accuracy. Security teams should also conduct periodic audits of their SIEM configurations to identify inefficiencies, reduce false positives, and enhance response workflows. As cyber threats evolve, SIEM systems must adapt by leveraging advanced analytics, artificial intelligence, and automation to keep pace with emerging attack techniques.

Real-time security monitoring is essential for protecting organizations from cyber threats by providing continuous visibility, rapid threat detection, and automated response capabilities. By leveraging log collection, event correlation, threat intelligence, and behavioral analytics, SIEM systems empower security teams to detect and mitigate security incidents before they escalate. As cyber threats become more sophisticated, organizations must invest in advanced SIEM capabilities to enhance their security operations and safeguard critical assets from evolving attack vectors.

Incident Detection and Response

Incident detection and response are critical components of an organization's cybersecurity strategy, ensuring that threats are identified and mitigated before they cause significant damage. Cyberattacks and security breaches are inevitable in today's digital landscape, making it essential for organizations to have robust mechanisms in place to detect and respond to incidents in real time. A Security Information and Event Management (SIEM) system plays a key role in this process by continuously monitoring security events, analyzing suspicious activities, and triggering alerts when potential threats are detected. Effective incident detection and response not only prevent financial and reputational losses but also ensure compliance with regulatory requirements.

Incident detection begins with the collection and analysis of security logs from multiple sources across an organization's IT infrastructure. Every device, application, and network component generates logs that contain valuable security information. Firewalls, intrusion detection systems, endpoint protection platforms, identity and access management solutions, and cloud security services all produce event data that can indicate potential threats. SIEM systems aggregate these logs, normalize the data, and correlate security events to identify anomalies. Without centralized log collection and real-time analysis, security teams would struggle to detect coordinated attack campaigns that span multiple systems and attack vectors.

Event correlation is one of the most important techniques used in incident detection. Cyberattacks often consist of multiple steps, where an attacker gains initial access, escalates privileges, moves laterally within the network, and ultimately exfiltrates data or deploys ransomware. Individually, these activities may not trigger alarms, but when correlated with other security events, they reveal a larger attack pattern. SIEM systems use correlation rules, machine learning algorithms, and threat intelligence feeds to detect multi-stage attacks. For example, a successful login from a compromised account followed by a data transfer to an external server could indicate data exfiltration. By linking these events together, SIEM helps security teams detect threats before attackers achieve their objectives.

Behavioral analytics further enhance incident detection by identifying deviations from normal activity. Traditional detection methods rely on static rules that define known attack patterns, but modern attackers frequently modify their techniques to evade signature-based defenses. User and entity behavior analytics (UEBA) incorporated into SIEM systems analyze patterns of user activity, system interactions, and network behavior to establish baselines for normal operations. When a deviation from these baselines occurs, such as a privileged user accessing critical files at unusual hours or an endpoint communicating with an unknown external domain, an alert is generated. This proactive approach enables security teams to detect insider threats, compromised credentials, and unknown malware infections that traditional security tools might overlook.

Threat intelligence integration plays a significant role in incident detection by providing real-time updates on known cyber threats, attack techniques, and malicious indicators. SIEM systems ingest threat intelligence feeds containing lists of suspicious IP addresses, domains, file hashes, and attacker tactics. When a security event matches an indicator of compromise (IOC) from a threat intelligence feed, the SIEM system generates an alert for further investigation. This allows organizations to identify threats early in the attack lifecycle and take action before the adversary can cause harm. Threat intelligence-driven detection also helps security teams distinguish between legitimate activity and known malicious behavior, reducing false positives and improving detection accuracy.

Incident response is the process of taking action after a security incident has been detected. A well-defined incident response plan ensures that organizations can contain and mitigate threats quickly, minimizing the impact on business operations. The incident response process typically follows a structured approach that includes detection, analysis, containment, eradication, recovery, and post-incident review.

When an alert is triggered in a SIEM system, security analysts assess the severity of the threat, gather relevant log data, and determine whether immediate action is necessary. Effective incident response requires collaboration between security teams, IT administrators, and executive leadership to ensure that threats are managed efficiently.

Automated response mechanisms significantly improve incident response times by enabling security teams to take immediate action against detected threats. SIEM systems integrate with Security Orchestration, Automation, and Response (SOAR) platforms to automate threat mitigation actions based on predefined workflows. For example, if a SIEM system detects a brute-force attack on a critical server, it can automatically block the attacking IP address, disable the targeted user account, and notify security analysts for further investigation. Automating response actions reduces the reliance on manual intervention, allowing organizations to contain threats before they spread within the network.

Isolation of compromised systems is a crucial step in incident response. When a security breach is detected, affected endpoints, servers, or user accounts must be isolated from the network to prevent the attacker from escalating privileges or exfiltrating data. SIEM-driven incident response workflows can automatically quarantine infected devices, restrict access to sensitive resources, and enforce multi-factor authentication for high-risk accounts. By isolating compromised assets, organizations limit the scope of an attack and prevent further damage while security teams investigate the root cause.

Incident response also involves forensic analysis to determine how the attack occurred and what data may have been compromised. Security analysts use SIEM logs and historical event data to reconstruct the attack timeline, identify vulnerabilities, and assess the impact of the breach. Forensic investigations help organizations understand attacker tactics, techniques, and procedures (TTPs), enabling them to improve security defenses and prevent similar incidents in the future. SIEM systems provide extensive logging and reporting capabilities that facilitate forensic analysis, allowing organizations to comply with regulatory requirements and support legal proceedings if necessary.

The final phase of incident response is recovery and post-incident review. Once the threat has been contained and eradicated, organizations must restore affected systems, reinforce security controls, and update policies to prevent recurrence. Security teams conduct post-incident reviews to evaluate the effectiveness of their response efforts, identify gaps in security defenses, and implement lessons learned. SIEM-generated reports help organizations analyze attack patterns, measure response times, and assess overall security resilience. By continuously refining incident response strategies, organizations can strengthen their cybersecurity posture and enhance their ability to respond to future threats.

Incident detection and response are essential for protecting organizations from cyber threats, data breaches, and operational disruptions. SIEM systems play a crucial role in enabling security teams to detect threats in real time, correlate security events, and execute automated response actions. By leveraging advanced analytics, behavioral monitoring, and threat intelligence integration, SIEM solutions empower organizations to stay ahead of evolving cyber threats. An effective incident detection and response strategy ensures that security teams can quickly identify attacks, contain threats, and recover from security incidents while minimizing damage to business operations.

SIEM Use Cases in Threat Detection

Security Information and Event Management (SIEM) systems are essential tools in modern cybersecurity, providing organizations with the ability to detect, analyze, and respond to threats in real time. SIEM solutions aggregate security data from multiple sources, correlate events, and generate alerts when suspicious activities are detected. Their effectiveness in threat detection is due to their ability to analyze large volumes of log data, apply advanced analytics, and integrate with threat intelligence sources. SIEM systems play a crucial role in identifying a wide range of cyber threats, from insider threats and brute-force attacks to advanced persistent threats (APTs) and malware infections. By leveraging SIEM technology, organizations can enhance their security posture and proactively defend against emerging threats.

One of the primary use cases of SIEM in threat detection is identifying brute-force attacks. Attackers frequently attempt to gain unauthorized access to systems by systematically guessing usernames and passwords. These attacks can be carried out using automated tools that rapidly try multiple credential combinations. SIEM solutions detect brute-force attacks by correlating multiple failed login attempts within a short time frame, followed by a successful login from the same source. When this pattern is identified, the SIEM system generates an alert, allowing security teams to investigate whether the login was legitimate or if an account has been compromised. Additionally, SIEM platforms can integrate with Security Orchestration, Automation, and Response (SOAR) tools to automatically block the attacker's IP address or enforce multi-factor authentication for the affected user.

Insider threat detection is another critical use case for SIEM systems. Unlike external threats, insider threats originate from employees, contractors, or third-party vendors who have legitimate access to an organization's systems and data. These individuals may misuse their privileges for financial gain, corporate espionage, or personal grievances. Detecting insider threats is challenging because traditional security tools focus on external attacks. SIEM systems address this issue by using User and Entity Behavior Analytics (UEBA) to establish normal user behavior and detect deviations. If an employee who typically accesses a limited set of files suddenly begins downloading large amounts of sensitive data, the SIEM system can flag this activity as anomalous. By continuously monitoring user activity and correlating it with access logs, file modifications, and privilege escalation attempts, SIEM solutions help organizations detect and prevent data leaks and unauthorized access.

SIEM platforms also play a crucial role in detecting phishing attacks. Phishing remains one of the most effective methods used by attackers to steal credentials and gain unauthorized access to corporate networks. Attackers send fraudulent emails that appear to be from legitimate sources, tricking users into providing login credentials or downloading malicious attachments. SIEM solutions help detect phishing attempts by analyzing email traffic, identifying known phishing domains, and correlating security events related to credential misuse. If a user enters their credentials on a phishing website and the same credentials are later used to log in from an unusual geographic location, the SIEM system can generate an alert. By integrating with email security gateways and threat intelligence feeds, SIEM solutions enhance an organization's ability to detect and respond to phishing campaigns.

Advanced Persistent Threats (APTs) are among the most dangerous and difficult-to-detect cyber threats. APTs involve highly skilled attackers who infiltrate networks and remain undetected for extended periods, often stealing sensitive data or disrupting critical operations. These attacks typically involve multiple stages, such as initial compromise, privilege escalation, lateral movement, and data exfiltration. SIEM systems detect APTs by correlating security events across different systems and identifying suspicious activity patterns. For example, a SIEM platform may detect an employee logging in from an unfamiliar location, followed by an attempt to access restricted files and then a sudden data transfer to an external server. By analyzing these activities collectively rather than in isolation, SIEM solutions can identify stealthy attack campaigns and alert security teams to potential threats.

Malware detection is another important use case for SIEM systems. Traditional antivirus solutions rely on signature-based detection methods, which are often ineffective against zero-day threats and polymorphic malware. SIEM solutions enhance malware detection by analyzing network traffic, file access patterns, and endpoint behaviors. If an endpoint begins exhibiting unusual activity, such as executing an unauthorized script, connecting to a known malicious domain, or modifying system files, the SIEM system can flag it as a potential malware infection. By correlating security events related to process execution, registry changes, and outbound network connections, SIEM platforms help security teams detect and contain malware outbreaks before they spread across the organization.

Ransomware detection is a growing concern for organizations worldwide. Ransomware attacks involve encrypting an organization's data and demanding payment in exchange for a decryption key. These attacks can cripple business operations and result in significant financial losses. SIEM systems detect ransomware attacks by identifying key indicators, such as a sudden increase in file encryption activities, unauthorized modifications to system backups, and communication with known ransomware command-and-control (C2) servers. By integrating with endpoint detection and response (EDR) solutions, SIEM platforms can automatically isolate infected systems, prevent further encryption, and notify security teams to initiate an incident response.

Cloud security monitoring has become an essential use case for SIEM solutions as organizations increasingly migrate to cloud environments. Cloud platforms generate massive amounts of security logs, including user access logs, API calls, and configuration changes. SIEM systems ingest and analyze these logs to detect unauthorized access attempts, privilege escalation, and data exfiltration from cloud storage services. If a user suddenly logs into a cloud management console from a previously unseen IP address and attempts to disable security controls, the SIEM system can flag the activity as suspicious. By correlating cloud security events with on-premises logs, SIEM solutions provide organizations with a unified view of their security posture across hybrid and multi-cloud environments.

Lateral movement detection is another key use case for SIEM systems. Once an attacker gains access to an organization's network, they often attempt to move laterally to access more sensitive systems and data. SIEM solutions detect lateral movement by analyzing authentication logs, monitoring failed access attempts to privileged accounts, and identifying unusual network traffic patterns. If a low-privilege account suddenly attempts to access an administrator's workstation or connect to a sensitive database, the SIEM system can generate an alert. By integrating with identity and access management (IAM) solutions, SIEM platforms can enforce stricter access controls and prevent unauthorized privilege escalation.

Data exfiltration detection is critical for preventing data breaches. Attackers often attempt to transfer sensitive data outside an organization through unauthorized file uploads, email attachments, or cloud storage services. SIEM solutions detect data exfiltration by monitoring file access logs, analyzing outbound network traffic, and identifying suspicious data transfers. If a workstation suddenly begins uploading large volumes of data to an unfamiliar domain, the SIEM system can alert security teams to investigate potential data theft. By combining network monitoring, anomaly detection, and endpoint behavior analysis, SIEM platforms help organizations prevent intellectual property theft and regulatory violations.

SIEM use cases in threat detection span a wide range of attack scenarios, from common threats like brute-force attacks and phishing to more sophisticated threats like APTs and ransomware. By leveraging event correlation, behavioral analytics, threat intelligence integration, and real-time monitoring, SIEM solutions provide organizations with powerful capabilities to detect and respond to cyber threats. As attack techniques continue to evolve, SIEM systems will play an increasingly important role in helping security teams stay ahead of cyber adversaries and protect critical digital assets.

Compliance and Regulatory Requirements

Compliance and regulatory requirements play a crucial role in modern cybersecurity, ensuring that organizations implement effective security measures to protect sensitive data and mitigate risks. Governments, industry regulators, and international bodies have established a range of standards and frameworks that organizations must follow to safeguard personal information, financial records, and intellectual property. Non-compliance with these regulations can result in severe penalties, legal action, and reputational damage. A Security Information and Event Management (SIEM) system is a critical tool for helping organizations meet compliance requirements by providing centralized log management, real-time monitoring, and automated reporting capabilities. By leveraging SIEM, organizations can demonstrate regulatory adherence, detect policy violations, and generate the necessary documentation for audits.

One of the most widely recognized compliance regulations is the General Data Protection Regulation (GDPR), which applies to organizations that process personal data of European Union (EU) citizens. GDPR mandates that organizations implement strict security controls to protect personal information, including encryption, access controls, and real-time monitoring of security incidents. Under GDPR, organizations must also report data breaches within 72 hours of discovery. A SIEM system enables organizations to track access to personal data, detect unauthorized access attempts, and generate detailed logs that can be used to investigate security incidents. By automating compliance reporting, SIEM helps organizations provide the necessary documentation to demonstrate adherence to GDPR requirements and avoid substantial fines.

The Health Insurance Portability and Accountability Act (HIPAA) is another critical regulatory framework that affects organizations in the healthcare sector. HIPAA requires healthcare providers, insurers, and business associates to protect patient health information (PHI) from unauthorized access, modification, and disclosure. Organizations must implement security controls to ensure the confidentiality, integrity, and availability of PHI. SIEM solutions play a key role in HIPAA compliance by monitoring access to electronic health records, detecting anomalies in user activity, and generating audit logs for security reviews. If an unauthorized user attempts to access patient records or if there are unusual patterns of data access, SIEM can alert security teams and prevent potential data breaches. By automating log retention and forensic analysis, SIEM ensures that organizations meet HIPAA's security and privacy requirements.

The Payment Card Industry Data Security Standard (PCI DSS) applies to organizations that handle credit card transactions, requiring them to implement strong security measures to protect payment data. PCI DSS mandates logging and monitoring of security events, network segmentation to separate payment processing systems from other parts of the network, and regular security assessments to identify vulnerabilities. SIEM helps organizations achieve PCI DSS compliance by collecting logs from firewalls, intrusion detection systems, and point-of-sale (POS) devices, allowing security teams to detect unauthorized access attempts or fraudulent transactions. By continuously monitoring network activity, SIEM solutions help prevent payment card fraud and provide the detailed audit trails required for PCI DSS compliance verification.

The Sarbanes-Oxley Act (SOX) is a U.S. federal law that establishes financial reporting and security requirements for publicly traded companies. SOX mandates that organizations implement security controls to protect financial records from tampering, unauthorized access, and fraud. Companies must maintain accurate logs of financial transactions, access controls, and security incidents to ensure compliance. SIEM supports SOX compliance by monitoring financial systems for suspicious activities, ensuring the integrity of financial data, and generating automated reports for auditors. If unauthorized changes are detected in financial databases or if there are attempts to bypass security controls, SIEM provides real-time alerts that help security teams take corrective action before financial data is compromised.

The Federal Information Security Management Act (FISMA) is a U.S. regulation that applies to government agencies and contractors, requiring them to implement risk-based security measures to protect sensitive information. FISMA mandates continuous monitoring of security events, risk assessments, and incident response planning. SIEM assists government organizations in meeting FISMA requirements by providing real-time visibility into security incidents, detecting unauthorized access attempts, and automating compliance reporting. By centralizing log management and providing detailed security analytics, SIEM solutions help federal agencies maintain compliance with FISMA and protect national security information from cyber threats.

The International Organization for Standardization (ISO) 27001 is a globally recognized information security standard that provides a framework for managing security risks and protecting sensitive data. Organizations seeking ISO 27001 certification must implement a comprehensive security management system that includes continuous monitoring, incident detection, and risk assessment. SIEM solutions support ISO 27001 compliance by providing automated monitoring of security events, detecting policy violations, and generating compliance reports. Organizations can use SIEM to enforce security policies, track access to critical systems, and ensure that security controls remain effective against evolving threats. By integrating SIEM with risk management frameworks, organizations can achieve ISO 27001 certification and demonstrate their commitment to information security best practices.

The National Institute of Standards and Technology (NIST) Cybersecurity Framework is a widely adopted set of guidelines designed to help organizations manage cybersecurity risks. NIST emphasizes five core functions: identify, protect, detect, respond, and recover. SIEM systems align with these principles by providing real-time threat detection, automated incident response, and forensic analysis capabilities. By leveraging SIEM, organizations can continuously monitor their security posture, detect policy violations, and implement corrective actions based on security event data. SIEM solutions also help organizations comply with other NIST-related standards, such as NIST 800-53, which outlines security controls for federal information systems.

Organizations operating in the financial sector must comply with regulations such as the Gramm-Leach-Bliley Act (GLBA) and the Financial Industry Regulatory Authority (FINRA) guidelines. These regulations require financial institutions to protect customer financial data, monitor transactions for fraudulent activity, and report security breaches. SIEM solutions play a critical role in financial compliance by analyzing transaction logs, detecting unauthorized access attempts, and preventing data leaks. By integrating with fraud detection systems and behavioral analytics tools, SIEM enhances an organization's ability to detect suspicious financial activities and ensure compliance with banking and financial regulations.

Regulatory requirements often mandate security teams to conduct regular audits and generate compliance reports to demonstrate adherence to security policies. SIEM solutions simplify the audit process by providing pre-configured compliance report templates, automated log retention, and searchable audit trails. Security teams can generate reports on user access, security incidents, and policy violations within seconds, reducing the manual effort required for compliance verification. Organizations can also use SIEM-generated reports to identify security gaps, refine incident response plans, and improve overall risk management strategies. By automating compliance reporting, SIEM enables organizations to meet regulatory deadlines and respond quickly to audit requests.

As cyber threats continue to evolve, regulatory requirements will become increasingly stringent, requiring organizations to adopt proactive security measures to protect sensitive data. SIEM solutions provide the necessary visibility, automation, and analytics to help organizations meet compliance obligations and strengthen their security posture. By continuously monitoring security events, detecting anomalies, and generating compliance reports, SIEM systems ensure that organizations remain compliant with industry regulations while effectively mitigating cybersecurity risks.

SIEM Architecture and Design Principles

The architecture and design of a Security Information and Event Management (SIEM) system play a critical role in its effectiveness, scalability, and reliability. SIEM solutions are designed to collect, process, analyze, and store vast amounts of security event data from multiple sources across an organization's IT infrastructure. The architecture of a SIEM system must support real-time monitoring, advanced analytics, and rapid incident response while ensuring seamless integration with existing security tools and technologies. A well-designed SIEM architecture provides organizations with centralized security visibility, threat detection capabilities, and compliance enforcement mechanisms. The underlying design principles of a SIEM system determine its ability to handle large-scale data ingestion, apply advanced correlation techniques, and deliver actionable insights to security teams.

A fundamental component of SIEM architecture is the log collection and aggregation layer, responsible for gathering security event data from various sources. Modern IT environments consist of firewalls, intrusion detection and prevention systems, endpoint protection platforms, cloud applications, identity and access management solutions, and network security tools, all of which generate security logs. The SIEM system must be capable of collecting logs from diverse sources in different formats, normalizing the data, and storing it in a centralized repository. Log collection methods may include agents installed on endpoints, API integrations with cloud services, syslog protocols for network devices, and direct database queries for application logs. The architecture must be designed to ensure high-speed log ingestion without data loss, allowing security teams to maintain comprehensive visibility into their organization's security posture.

Once logs are collected, the SIEM system processes and normalizes them to create a standardized data format. Different security tools generate logs with unique structures, field names, and timestamps, making it difficult to correlate security events across multiple sources.

The normalization process converts raw logs into a consistent schema, extracting critical attributes such as event type, user identity, source and destination IP addresses, timestamps, and severity levels. This structured approach enables efficient searching, filtering, and correlation of security events, ensuring that security analysts can quickly identify and investigate incidents. The SIEM architecture must support scalable data processing capabilities to handle increasing log volumes generated by modern cloud environments, Internet of Things (IoT) devices, and remote workforces.

Event correlation is a core design principle of SIEM architecture, allowing security teams to detect complex attack patterns that may not be evident when analyzing individual security events in isolation. Correlation engines within the SIEM system apply predefined rules, behavioral analytics, and machine learning techniques to identify suspicious activities. The SIEM architecture must support real-time correlation to detect ongoing threats as they unfold, as well as historical correlation for forensic investigations. A well-designed SIEM system provides flexible correlation rule creation, enabling organizations to customize detection logic based on their specific security requirements. Correlation rules can link multiple related events, such as failed login attempts followed by privilege escalation, data exfiltration attempts, or lateral movement within the network.

Scalability is a key consideration in SIEM architecture, particularly for large enterprises that generate billions of security events daily. Traditional on-premises SIEM solutions often face limitations in handling high data volumes, leading to performance bottlenecks and delayed threat detection. Modern SIEM architectures leverage cloud-native infrastructures that provide dynamic scalability, distributed processing, and big data analytics. Cloud-based SIEM solutions enable organizations to scale their log storage and analysis capabilities based on demand, ensuring that security monitoring remains efficient even as IT environments grow in complexity. The SIEM architecture must support elastic scaling, allowing organizations to expand data ingestion, processing power, and retention capacity without affecting system performance.

Threat intelligence integration is an essential design principle in SIEM architecture, enhancing the system's ability to detect known and emerging threats. SIEM solutions ingest external threat intelligence feeds that provide real-time updates on malicious IP addresses, domains, attack signatures, and adversary tactics. By correlating internal security events with external threat intelligence, SIEM systems can identify indicators of compromise (IOCs) and detect threats that align with known attack patterns. The architecture must support automated threat intelligence ingestion, enrichment, and application to security event data, ensuring that organizations stay ahead of evolving cyber threats.

The incident response and automation layer of SIEM architecture plays a crucial role in mitigating security incidents quickly and effectively. Traditional SIEM systems primarily focused on alerting security teams when threats were detected, but modern SIEM architectures integrate with Security Orchestration, Automation, and Response (SOAR) platforms to automate response actions. Automated incident response capabilities allow SIEM solutions to take predefined actions, such as isolating compromised endpoints, blocking malicious IP addresses, disabling compromised user accounts, or triggering security policy updates. The architecture must support seamless integration with other security tools, such as endpoint detection and response (EDR), identity and access management (IAM), and firewall management systems, enabling coordinated threat mitigation efforts.

Data retention and storage management are critical design considerations in SIEM architecture, particularly for regulatory compliance and forensic investigations. Many industry regulations, such as GDPR, HIPAA, PCI DSS, and SOX, require organizations to retain security logs for extended periods to support compliance reporting and audit requirements. SIEM solutions must efficiently store and index historical logs while ensuring that they remain searchable and accessible for security analysis. The architecture must balance long-term storage needs with performance optimization, utilizing tiered storage approaches that differentiate between frequently accessed data and archived logs. Cloud-based SIEM solutions often employ distributed storage technologies to accommodate high data retention demands while minimizing infrastructure costs.

Security and access control mechanisms within SIEM architecture ensure that only authorized personnel can access sensitive security data and configuration settings. The SIEM system must implement role-based access control (RBAC), multi-factor authentication (MFA), and encryption mechanisms to protect security event data from unauthorized access. Security analysts, compliance officers, and IT administrators must have different levels of access based on their responsibilities, ensuring that sensitive threat intelligence and forensic investigation data remain protected. The architecture must also include audit logging capabilities that track all actions performed within the SIEM system, allowing organizations to detect and investigate any unauthorized modifications or data access attempts.

User experience and operational efficiency are important factors in SIEM design, ensuring that security teams can efficiently monitor threats and investigate incidents. A well-designed SIEM system provides intuitive dashboards, real-time visualizations, and customizable reporting features that enable security analysts to quickly assess the organization's security posture. The SIEM architecture must support advanced search functionalities, allowing analysts to filter security event data based on various attributes such as event severity, user identity, and network traffic patterns. The inclusion of artificial intelligence and machine learning-driven analytics further enhances SIEM usability, helping analysts prioritize high-risk threats and reduce false positives.

The overall architecture and design principles of a SIEM system determine its ability to provide real-time threat detection, scalable log management, and automated response capabilities. A robust SIEM architecture integrates seamlessly with existing security tools, supports high-speed data ingestion and processing, and applies advanced correlation techniques to detect complex cyber threats. As organizations continue to face an evolving threat landscape, SIEM solutions must be designed with flexibility, scalability, and automation in mind to effectively protect critical digital assets and maintain regulatory compliance.

Choosing the Right SIEM Solution

Selecting the right Security Information and Event Management (SIEM) solution is a critical decision for any organization seeking to enhance its security posture, detect cyber threats, and ensure regulatory compliance. The SIEM market offers a wide range of solutions, each with different capabilities, architectures, and pricing models. Organizations must carefully evaluate their specific security requirements, budget constraints, and operational needs before choosing a SIEM platform. A well-chosen SIEM solution provides real-time security monitoring, advanced threat detection, automated response capabilities, and seamless integration with existing security tools. Understanding the key factors that influence SIEM selection helps organizations make informed decisions and maximize the return on investment in cybersecurity.

One of the most important considerations when selecting a SIEM solution is scalability. Organizations generate vast amounts of security event data from network devices, endpoints, cloud environments, and business applications. A SIEM system must be capable of handling large volumes of log data while maintaining high performance and real-time analysis capabilities. Traditional on-premises SIEM solutions often struggle with scalability due to infrastructure limitations, whereas cloud-based SIEM platforms offer elastic scalability, allowing organizations to expand data processing capabilities as their IT environments grow. Choosing a SIEM that supports scalable log ingestion and processing ensures that security teams can maintain continuous visibility without performance degradation.

Log collection and integration capabilities are another crucial factor in SIEM selection. Organizations use a variety of security tools, including firewalls, intrusion detection systems, endpoint protection platforms, identity and access management (IAM) solutions, and threat intelligence feeds. A SIEM system must support integration with all these sources to provide a comprehensive view of security events. Some SIEM solutions require proprietary log formats, making it difficult to ingest data from third-party tools. The ideal SIEM platform should support standardized log formats, such as syslog, JSON, and Common Event Format (CEF), to facilitate seamless data collection and normalization. Evaluating the SIEM's ability to integrate with existing security infrastructure ensures that organizations can aggregate and analyze security events efficiently.

Threat detection and correlation capabilities play a key role in the effectiveness of a SIEM solution. The ability to detect multi-stage attacks, correlate related security events, and provide contextual threat intelligence determines the SIEM's value in security operations. Traditional rule-based SIEM systems rely on predefined correlation rules, which require continuous updates to stay effective against evolving threats. Modern SIEM platforms incorporate machine learning and behavioral analytics to identify anomalies and detect previously unknown attack patterns. Evaluating a SIEM's correlation engine, artificial intelligence capabilities, and support for User and Entity Behavior Analytics (UEBA) helps organizations determine how effectively the solution can identify sophisticated cyber threats.

Real-time alerting and incident response automation are essential features of a SIEM solution. Security teams rely on SIEM-generated alerts to detect and respond to threats before they escalate. A SIEM system should provide customizable alerting mechanisms that prioritize critical threats while minimizing false positives. Integration with Security Orchestration, Automation, and Response (SOAR) platforms enhances a SIEM's ability to automate threat mitigation actions, such as isolating compromised endpoints, blocking malicious IP addresses, and enforcing security policies. Evaluating the SIEM's alerting mechanisms, response automation capabilities, and integration with existing security workflows helps organizations enhance their incident response efficiency.

Compliance and reporting features are also critical when choosing a SIEM solution. Many industries are subject to strict regulatory requirements, such as GDPR, HIPAA, PCI DSS, and SOX, which mandate security event monitoring, log retention, and audit reporting. A SIEM system should provide built-in compliance reporting templates, automated log retention policies, and real-time auditing capabilities to simplify regulatory adherence. Some SIEM solutions include compliance dashboards that enable security teams to generate reports with minimal manual effort. Organizations must assess whether the SIEM solution supports their specific compliance needs and provides the necessary tools to streamline audit preparation and documentation.

Deployment flexibility is another factor to consider when evaluating SIEM solutions. Organizations have different infrastructure requirements, ranging from on-premises data centers to hybrid and multi-cloud environments. Some SIEM solutions are designed for on-premises deployment, requiring organizations to manage hardware, software, and maintenance. Others offer cloud-based SIEM models, which reduce infrastructure overhead and provide greater flexibility in data storage and processing. Hybrid SIEM solutions allow organizations to maintain on-premises log collection while leveraging cloud-based analytics and threat intelligence. Selecting a SIEM deployment model that aligns with an organization's infrastructure strategy ensures optimal performance and cost efficiency.

Cost and licensing models play a significant role in SIEM selection. Traditional SIEM solutions often use volume-based pricing, where costs are determined by the amount of log data ingested and stored. This pricing model can become expensive as log volumes increase, making it difficult for organizations to predict costs. Cloud-based SIEM providers often offer subscription-based pricing with predictable costs, while some modern solutions use event-based pricing models that charge based on the number of security events analyzed rather than raw log volume. Organizations must carefully evaluate SIEM pricing structures, considering factors such as licensing fees, storage costs, and operational expenses to ensure cost-effectiveness.

Ease of use and operational efficiency are critical considerations for security teams that manage SIEM platforms. Some SIEM solutions require extensive manual configuration, fine-tuning of correlation rules, and continuous maintenance, which can place a heavy burden on security teams. Other SIEM platforms offer intuitive dashboards, automated rule creation, and AI-driven recommendations that reduce the complexity of managing security events. Evaluating the SIEM's user interface, search functionality, dashboard customization options, and automation features helps organizations determine whether the solution aligns with their security team's capabilities and resources.

Vendor reputation and customer support are also important factors when selecting a SIEM solution. Established SIEM vendors with a strong track record in the cybersecurity industry provide greater reliability, regular software updates, and continuous threat intelligence integration. Organizations should assess vendor support options, including 24/7 technical assistance, training resources, and managed SIEM services. Some SIEM providers offer managed detection and response (MDR) services that supplement in-house security operations with expert threat analysis and incident response support. Evaluating vendor support, service-level agreements (SLAs), and customer feedback helps organizations choose a SIEM provider that offers long-term reliability and ongoing security enhancements.

Selecting the right SIEM solution requires a thorough evaluation of scalability, integration capabilities, threat detection features, compliance support, deployment flexibility, cost structure, ease of use, and vendor reputation. Organizations must align their SIEM selection with their security goals, regulatory requirements, and operational needs to ensure effective security monitoring and incident response. By choosing a SIEM platform that provides real-time threat intelligence, automated response capabilities, and seamless integration with existing security tools, organizations can enhance their cybersecurity posture and stay ahead of evolving cyber threats.

Open-Source vs. Commercial SIEM Systems

Organizations looking to implement a Security Information and Event Management (SIEM) system must choose between open-source and commercial solutions. Both options offer distinct advantages and challenges, and the decision largely depends on factors such as budget, scalability, security requirements, and available in-house expertise. Open-source SIEM solutions provide flexibility and cost savings, making them attractive to organizations with technical expertise that can handle customization and maintenance. Commercial SIEM solutions, on the other hand, offer advanced threat detection, automation, dedicated support, and integration with enterprise security tools, making them a preferred choice for organizations that require a fully managed, scalable security monitoring solution. Understanding the differences between these two types of SIEM systems is essential for selecting the best solution to meet an organization's security and operational needs.

One of the most significant advantages of open-source SIEM systems is cost efficiency. Unlike commercial SIEM solutions that require expensive licensing fees and subscription costs, open-source SIEM platforms are freely available for download and deployment. Organizations with limited cybersecurity budgets can leverage open-source SIEM tools without incurring high upfront costs. However, while the software itself is free, implementing and maintaining an open-source SIEM system requires skilled personnel who can configure, optimize, and manage the platform. Organizations must factor in the costs of hiring or training security professionals to operate an open-source SIEM effectively. Without proper expertise, organizations may struggle to configure the system correctly, leading to misconfigurations and security gaps.

Customization and flexibility are key strengths of open-source SIEM solutions. Organizations that require a highly tailored security monitoring system can modify open-source SIEM platforms to fit their specific needs. These solutions offer complete access to the source code, allowing security teams to develop custom correlation rules, dashboards, and integrations with other security tools. Open-source SIEM systems are ideal for organizations with unique security requirements that are not fully addressed by commercial products. However, the customization process requires a deep understanding of coding, scripting, and security analytics, making open-source SIEM platforms less suitable for organizations without strong technical expertise.

Scalability is a crucial consideration when choosing between open-source and commercial SIEM solutions. Open-source SIEM systems often require additional infrastructure and manual tuning to scale effectively as an organization grows. Large enterprises generating vast amounts of log data may find it challenging to maintain the performance of an open-source SIEM solution without investing in high-performance storage and processing capabilities. Commercial SIEM providers offer cloud-based and hybrid deployment options that allow organizations to scale effortlessly as their security monitoring needs increase. Cloud-native SIEM solutions provide elastic scalability, distributed data processing, and high availability, ensuring that security teams can monitor large volumes of security events in real time without performance degradation.

Threat detection and analytics capabilities vary significantly between open-source and commercial SIEM platforms. Open-source SIEM solutions typically offer basic event correlation and log analysis features, but they often lack advanced machine learning-driven analytics, behavioral threat detection, and automated response capabilities. Commercial SIEM solutions incorporate artificial intelligence and user behavior analytics to detect sophisticated cyber threats, reduce false positives, and improve incident response efficiency. Organizations that require advanced threat intelligence integration, anomaly detection, and automated risk scoring may find that commercial SIEM platforms provide a more robust security monitoring framework than open-source alternatives.

Integration with third-party security tools is another factor that differentiates open-source and commercial SIEM systems. Open-source SIEM solutions may require manual configuration to integrate with firewalls, endpoint protection platforms, identity management systems, and cloud security tools. Security teams must develop custom scripts and connectors to ingest logs from various sources and ensure seamless data normalization. In contrast, commercial SIEM solutions offer pre-built integrations with a wide range of security tools, enabling organizations to deploy a fully integrated security monitoring system with minimal configuration. Commercial SIEM platforms also provide built-in connectors for cloud environments such as AWS, Azure, and Google Cloud, simplifying log ingestion and threat detection across hybrid infrastructures.

Support and maintenance are critical considerations when selecting a SIEM system. Open-source SIEM solutions rely on community support, online forums, and documentation for troubleshooting and updates. While the open-source community provides valuable resources, organizations using open-source SIEM platforms must dedicate internal resources to system maintenance, security patching, and software updates. Commercial SIEM solutions offer dedicated customer support, including 24/7 assistance, security advisory services, and proactive threat intelligence updates. Organizations that require immediate support and regular updates to stay ahead of evolving threats may benefit from the reliability of a commercial SIEM vendor.

Compliance and regulatory requirements also play a role in the choice between open-source and commercial SIEM solutions. Many organizations must adhere to industry-specific regulations such as GDPR, HIPAA, PCI DSS, and SOX, which mandate security monitoring, log retention, and incident reporting. Commercial SIEM solutions provide built-in compliance reporting tools, automated log archiving, and pre-configured dashboards that simplify regulatory adherence. Open-source SIEM solutions may require additional customization and manual report generation to meet compliance requirements, increasing the complexity of audit preparation and regulatory reporting.

Performance optimization is another area where commercial SIEM solutions have an advantage over open-source platforms. Commercial SIEM vendors continuously optimize their platforms for high-speed data processing, real-time threat correlation, and efficient log storage. Open-source SIEM solutions, while powerful, may require significant manual tuning to optimize query performance, reduce false positives, and enhance data indexing. Organizations that prioritize real-time threat detection and low-latency log analysis may find that commercial SIEM solutions offer better performance out of the box.

Organizations must also consider the long-term sustainability of their SIEM investment. Open-source SIEM solutions provide freedom from vendor lock-in, allowing organizations to modify and extend the platform as needed. However, maintaining an open-source SIEM system over the long term requires continuous development, in-house expertise, and ongoing infrastructure management. Commercial SIEM solutions, while requiring licensing fees, provide long-term support, security updates, and new feature enhancements, ensuring that organizations can keep pace with evolving cybersecurity challenges.

Choosing between open-source and commercial SIEM solutions depends on an organization's security needs, available resources, compliance requirements, and long-term goals. Open-source SIEM platforms offer cost savings, customization, and flexibility but require significant technical expertise and ongoing maintenance. Commercial

SIEM solutions provide advanced threat detection, scalability, automation, and dedicated support, making them ideal for organizations that require a fully managed security monitoring solution. By carefully evaluating the advantages and limitations of each approach, organizations can select a SIEM system that aligns with their security strategy and operational capabilities.

SIEM Deployment Planning

Deploying a Security Information and Event Management (SIEM) system requires careful planning to ensure that it meets the organization's security, compliance, and operational requirements. SIEM solutions provide centralized log management, real-time threat detection, and automated incident response, making them essential for modern cybersecurity strategies. However, a poorly planned SIEM deployment can lead to performance issues, high operational costs, and ineffective threat detection. Organizations must define their objectives, assess their existing security infrastructure, and develop a structured deployment strategy to maximize the effectiveness of their SIEM system.

The first step in SIEM deployment planning is defining the organization's security and compliance requirements. Different industries and regulatory frameworks impose specific security monitoring and log retention obligations. Organizations handling sensitive customer data, financial records, or healthcare information must ensure that their SIEM system complies with regulations such as GDPR, HIPAA, PCI DSS, and SOX. Security teams should identify the types of security events that need to be monitored, the required retention periods for logs, and the reporting capabilities needed to meet audit and compliance requirements. Establishing these requirements at the outset ensures that the chosen SIEM solution aligns with the organization's legal and security obligations.

Scoping the deployment is the next crucial step in planning a SIEM implementation. Organizations must determine which assets, systems, and applications need to be monitored. This includes defining the log sources that will be integrated with the SIEM system, such as firewalls, intrusion detection and prevention systems, endpoint protection platforms, identity management solutions, cloud services, and database servers. Identifying high-risk assets and critical business applications ensures that the SIEM system prioritizes monitoring and alerting for the most valuable resources. Security teams must also assess network topology and data flow to determine how logs will be collected from distributed environments, including remote offices and cloud-based infrastructures.

Choosing the right deployment model is an important decision in SIEM planning. Organizations can select from on-premises, cloud-based, or hybrid SIEM solutions based on their security architecture and operational needs. On-premises SIEM deployments offer full control over data storage, processing, and security policies, making them suitable for organizations with strict data privacy requirements. However, on-premises SIEM solutions require significant infrastructure investment, ongoing maintenance, and dedicated personnel to manage log ingestion, correlation, and threat analysis. Cloud-based SIEM solutions provide scalability, reduced infrastructure costs, and automatic updates, making them ideal for organizations that need a flexible and low-maintenance security monitoring solution. Hybrid SIEM deployments combine on-premises and cloud-based components, enabling organizations to retain critical logs in their data centers while leveraging cloud analytics for advanced threat detection.

Selecting the appropriate log collection method is another key aspect of SIEM deployment planning. Organizations generate large volumes of security logs from various sources, and efficient log collection ensures that critical security events are not missed. SIEM solutions support multiple log collection methods, including agent-based collection, API integration, syslog forwarding, and network-based event monitoring. Agent-based collection involves deploying lightweight software agents on endpoints and servers to gather logs and send them to the SIEM system. API-based collection allows SIEM solutions to retrieve security logs from cloud services, SaaS applications, and third-party security tools. Organizations must choose the most efficient log collection methods based on their network architecture, data sources, and security monitoring requirements.

Log normalization and parsing must be considered during the planning phase to ensure that security events from different sources can be correlated effectively. Various security tools generate logs in different formats, making it essential to standardize log data for accurate analysis. SIEM systems use normalization techniques to convert raw log entries into a common format, ensuring consistency in data structure and field mappings. Organizations should work with security teams and SIEM vendors to define parsing rules that extract relevant attributes, such as timestamps, user identities, source and destination IP addresses, event types, and severity levels. Proper log normalization enhances the SIEM system's ability to detect patterns, analyze threats, and generate meaningful alerts.

Event correlation rules and alerting thresholds should be configured as part of the SIEM deployment plan. Security teams must define correlation logic that links multiple related security events to identify potential threats. For example, a failed login attempt followed by a successful authentication from an unfamiliar IP address may indicate a credential-based attack. Configuring correlation rules ensures that the SIEM system accurately detects threats while minimizing false positives. Organizations should also establish alerting thresholds that prioritize high-risk incidents while reducing noise from low-priority security events. Fine-tuning correlation and alerting settings over time helps improve the accuracy and effectiveness of threat detection.

Performance optimization is a critical consideration in SIEM deployment. SIEM solutions must process vast amounts of log data in real time while maintaining high performance and low latency. Organizations should allocate sufficient compute resources, storage capacity, and network bandwidth to handle the expected volume of security events. Implementing a tiered storage approach can improve efficiency by storing frequently accessed logs on high-performance storage while archiving older logs in cost-effective long-term storage. Cloud-based SIEM platforms often provide auto-scaling capabilities to accommodate increased log ingestion and analysis workloads dynamically. Planning for scalability ensures that the SIEM system remains responsive as data volumes grow over time.

Incident response integration should be part of SIEM deployment planning to ensure that security teams can act quickly when threats are detected. SIEM solutions must integrate with Security Orchestration, Automation, and Response (SOAR) platforms, ticketing systems, and security workflows to streamline incident investigation and remediation. Automated response actions, such as blocking malicious IP addresses, quarantining compromised devices, and enforcing access controls, should be defined within the SIEM platform. Security teams should also establish playbooks and escalation procedures that guide analysts through the process of assessing, containing, and mitigating security incidents. Integrating SIEM with existing security operations workflows improves response efficiency and reduces the risk of cyberattacks escalating.

Testing and validation are essential before fully deploying a SIEM system into production. Organizations should conduct pilot deployments in controlled environments to verify log ingestion, correlation rule accuracy, and alerting effectiveness. Security teams should simulate attack scenarios, such as brute-force login attempts, malware infections, and insider threats, to evaluate how well the SIEM system detects and responds to security incidents. Fine-tuning log collection settings, correlation rules, and alerting thresholds based on test results helps improve SIEM performance and detection accuracy. Continuous monitoring and feedback loops should be established to refine configurations and adapt to evolving threats.

Ongoing maintenance and optimization should be factored into the SIEM deployment plan to ensure long-term effectiveness. Security teams must regularly update correlation rules, review alerting policies, and fine-tune log retention settings based on new security trends and compliance requirements. Regular audits should be conducted to identify gaps in log coverage, detect misconfigurations, and enhance threat detection capabilities. SIEM systems should also be integrated with threat intelligence feeds to stay updated with the latest indicators of compromise and emerging attack techniques. Organizations must allocate resources for continuous monitoring, system updates, and personnel training to maintain an effective and resilient SIEM deployment.

Proper planning is the foundation of a successful SIEM deployment, ensuring that organizations can detect, analyze, and respond to security threats effectively. By defining security objectives, selecting the right deployment model, optimizing log collection and correlation rules, and integrating automated response mechanisms, organizations can maximize the value of their SIEM investment. Ongoing testing, optimization, and maintenance efforts further enhance SIEM performance, allowing security teams to stay ahead of evolving cyber threats and maintain a strong security posture.

SIEM System Sizing and Scalability

The sizing and scalability of a Security Information and Event Management (SIEM) system are critical factors in ensuring its efficiency, performance, and ability to handle increasing security data volumes. Organizations generate massive amounts of security logs daily from various sources, including firewalls, intrusion detection systems, endpoint protection tools, cloud environments, and application servers. A well-sized SIEM system must be capable of ingesting, processing, and analyzing these logs in real time while maintaining optimal performance. Without proper planning for scalability, organizations risk experiencing performance bottlenecks, delayed threat detection, and inefficient storage management.

Properly sizing a SIEM system begins with understanding the volume of log data generated across an organization's IT infrastructure. Log volume depends on several factors, such as the number of devices, applications, users, and network activity levels. Security logs vary in size and frequency, with some devices generating small log entries every few minutes while others produce large volumes of logs continuously. Organizations must estimate their average log generation rate, measured in events per second (EPS), to determine the required processing capacity of their SIEM solution. EPS calculations help security teams understand how much data the SIEM system needs to process in real time to avoid performance degradation.

The next consideration in SIEM sizing is data retention requirements. Organizations must store logs for compliance, forensic investigations, and historical trend analysis. Regulatory frameworks such as GDPR, HIPAA, PCI DSS, and SOX mandate that security logs be retained for specific periods, ranging from months to years. Storing high volumes of security logs requires careful planning of storage capacity, indexing strategies, and retrieval performance. SIEM solutions must balance short-term high-performance storage for real-time analysis with long-term archival storage for compliance and auditing purposes.

Implementing tiered storage solutions, where recent logs are stored on high-speed storage and older logs are archived in cost-efficient cloud storage, optimizes data retention while managing costs.

Scalability is a fundamental aspect of SIEM deployment, ensuring that the system can grow as the organization expands its IT infrastructure. Traditional on-premises SIEM solutions often face challenges in scaling due to hardware limitations, requiring organizations to invest in additional servers, storage devices, and network resources. Cloud-based SIEM solutions offer greater scalability by leveraging distributed computing, allowing organizations to scale security monitoring capabilities dynamically based on demand. Hybrid SIEM deployments combine on-premises log collection with cloud-based analytics, providing flexibility and ensuring scalability without significant hardware investments.

SIEM scalability also depends on its ability to distribute processing workloads efficiently. As log volumes increase, SIEM solutions must handle data ingestion, correlation, and threat detection in a distributed manner. Load balancing mechanisms ensure that no single component of the SIEM system becomes overwhelmed by high data volumes. Modern SIEM architectures use distributed processing frameworks, such as big data technologies and parallel computing, to process security events across multiple nodes. This distributed approach enables SIEM solutions to analyze millions of security events per second without delays, ensuring real-time threat detection and incident response.

Indexing and search performance are critical in ensuring that a SIEM system remains scalable. Security analysts rely on SIEM platforms to perform searches, run queries, and conduct forensic investigations on historical log data. As data volumes grow, inefficient indexing mechanisms can slow down search operations, making it difficult to retrieve relevant security events quickly. SIEM solutions must implement optimized indexing techniques, such as time-based partitioning and compressed storage formats, to improve query performance. Cloud-based SIEM platforms often leverage advanced indexing technologies to enable near-instant search capabilities across vast log repositories.

High availability and fault tolerance are essential considerations in SIEM scalability planning. Security monitoring cannot afford downtime, as cyber threats can emerge at any moment. Organizations must ensure that their SIEM systems have built-in redundancy, failover mechanisms, and disaster recovery capabilities to maintain continuous security operations. Cloud-based SIEM solutions offer automatic failover and geographically distributed data centers to ensure uninterrupted service availability. On-premises SIEM deployments must implement redundant hardware, clustering, and backup strategies to prevent data loss in case of system failures.

Automated log filtering and data compression techniques contribute to SIEM scalability by reducing the storage and processing burden. Not all logs are equally valuable for security analysis, and filtering out unnecessary logs prevents the SIEM system from being overloaded with redundant data. Organizations can define log filtering policies to prioritize critical security events while discarding or archiving low-priority logs. Data compression techniques further optimize storage by reducing the size of stored log entries, allowing organizations to retain more historical data without consuming excessive storage resources.

Threat intelligence integration plays a role in SIEM scalability by ensuring that security events are enriched with relevant threat context without overwhelming the system. SIEM solutions integrate with external threat intelligence feeds to enhance detection capabilities by correlating internal security events with known indicators of compromise (IOCs). To prevent excessive data processing overhead, SIEM systems must intelligently apply threat intelligence to only the most relevant security events, avoiding unnecessary performance strain. Organizations should evaluate the impact of threat intelligence feeds on system scalability and ensure that they are optimized for efficiency.

SIEM scalability planning must also consider compliance with future data growth projections. Organizations continuously expand their IT environments by adopting new cloud services, IoT devices, and remote work solutions. Each of these technologies generates additional security logs that must be ingested and analyzed by the SIEM system. Security teams should conduct periodic scalability assessments to determine whether their SIEM deployment can handle increased log volumes and evolving security requirements. Proactive planning allows organizations to upgrade storage capacity, processing power, and network bandwidth as needed without disrupting security operations.

Operational efficiency is another factor in SIEM sizing, as security teams must be able to manage and interpret SIEM alerts effectively. A scalable SIEM solution must include automation features that reduce manual intervention, such as alert prioritization, correlation rule optimization, and machine learning-based anomaly detection. As SIEM log volumes increase, excessive false positives can overwhelm security analysts, making it difficult to identify real threats. Implementing advanced analytics and automated response mechanisms ensures that the SIEM system remains scalable without creating alert fatigue for security teams.

Capacity planning tools and performance monitoring solutions help organizations track the scalability of their SIEM deployment over time. Organizations should continuously monitor system performance metrics such as EPS rates, storage utilization, query response times, and alert generation efficiency. Performance tuning adjustments, such as optimizing correlation rules, refining data retention policies, and adjusting processing thresholds, help maintain SIEM efficiency as data volumes grow. Continuous optimization ensures that the SIEM system remains scalable, responsive, and capable of detecting threats in an evolving cybersecurity landscape.

Proper SIEM system sizing and scalability planning ensure that organizations can effectively monitor, analyze, and respond to security events as their IT environments expand. By evaluating log volumes, selecting the right deployment model, implementing distributed processing techniques, and optimizing storage and indexing, organizations can maintain a high-performance SIEM system capable of handling future security challenges. Organizations that proactively address scalability considerations ensure that their SIEM platform remains an essential component of their cybersecurity strategy, providing real-time visibility and threat intelligence without compromising performance.

Data Sources and Log Aggregation

A Security Information and Event Management (SIEM) system relies on data sources and log aggregation to provide real-time visibility into an organization's security posture. Logs contain valuable insights into network activity, user behavior, authentication attempts, and system events. By aggregating logs from multiple sources, SIEM solutions enable security teams to detect threats, analyze security incidents, and maintain compliance with regulatory requirements. Effective log aggregation ensures that all relevant security data is collected, normalized, and correlated to provide a holistic view of security operations. Organizations must carefully select data sources, configure log collection methods, and optimize storage to ensure that their SIEM system operates efficiently.

The primary data sources for SIEM include network devices, firewalls, intrusion detection and prevention systems (IDS/IPS), endpoint security tools, cloud services, authentication systems, and application logs. Network devices such as routers, switches, and load balancers generate logs that provide information about network traffic, packet flows, and access control policies. These logs help security teams identify unusual network activity, detect unauthorized access attempts, and monitor for signs of lateral movement by attackers. Firewalls generate logs that record incoming and outgoing traffic, blocked connections, and rule violations. By analyzing firewall logs, SIEM solutions can identify port scanning attempts, brute-force attacks, and suspicious outbound connections that may indicate data exfiltration.

Intrusion detection and prevention systems play a crucial role in identifying potential threats at the network perimeter. IDS logs capture suspicious traffic patterns, anomaly detections, and attempted exploits, while IPS logs record actions taken to block malicious activity. By aggregating IDS/IPS logs within a SIEM system, security teams can correlate threat indicators with other security events to detect coordinated attacks. Endpoint security tools, including antivirus software, endpoint detection and response (EDR) solutions, and operating system logs, provide visibility into user activity, file modifications, and malware infections. Endpoint logs help security teams detect unauthorized software installations, ransomware attacks, and privilege escalation attempts that could compromise critical assets.

Cloud services generate extensive security logs that must be aggregated into a SIEM system for comprehensive monitoring. Organizations using Amazon Web Services (AWS), Microsoft Azure, or Google Cloud Platform (GCP) must collect logs from cloud security tools, virtual machines, API calls, and identity and access management (IAM) systems. Cloud security logs provide insights into authentication attempts, configuration changes, data transfers, and user activity within cloud environments. Aggregating cloud logs in a SIEM platform ensures that security teams can monitor cloud infrastructure alongside on-premises systems, identifying threats such as unauthorized access, misconfigurations, and data breaches.

Authentication and access control logs provide critical information about user activity, login attempts, and privilege escalations. Identity and access management (IAM) solutions, directory services like Active Directory (AD), and single sign-on (SSO) platforms generate authentication logs that track user logins, failed login attempts, and account lockouts. SIEM systems analyze authentication logs to detect anomalous login behavior, such as multiple failed attempts followed by successful access from a suspicious location. By correlating authentication logs with network activity and endpoint security data, SIEM solutions help security teams detect compromised accounts, insider threats, and unauthorized privilege escalations.

Application logs are another essential data source for SIEM systems. Business applications, web servers, databases, and software-as-a-service (SaaS) platforms generate logs that provide visibility into user interactions, transaction history, and application errors. Web server logs capture HTTP requests, error responses, and user session activity, helping security teams identify web-based attacks such as SQL injection, cross-site scripting (XSS), and unauthorized API access. Database logs record queries, data modifications, and access attempts, enabling organizations to detect unauthorized data extraction and potential breaches. Aggregating application logs in a SIEM system ensures that security teams can monitor critical business processes and detect anomalies that may indicate application-layer attacks.

Log aggregation involves collecting, normalizing, and storing security logs from various sources in a centralized SIEM repository. Organizations must implement efficient log collection mechanisms to ensure that all relevant security events are captured without data loss. SIEM solutions support multiple log collection methods, including agent-based collection, syslog forwarding, API integration, and network-based monitoring. Agent-based log collection involves deploying lightweight software agents on endpoints, servers, and cloud workloads to collect security logs in real time. These agents transmit logs to the SIEM system over encrypted channels, ensuring secure data transfer. Syslog forwarding enables network devices, firewalls, and IDS/IPS solutions to send logs to a centralized SIEM system for processing and analysis.

API integration is essential for aggregating logs from cloud services, SaaS applications, and third-party security tools. Many cloud providers and security vendors offer API-based log retrieval mechanisms that allow SIEM solutions to pull security events directly from cloud platforms. Organizations using API-based log collection must ensure that their SIEM system supports automated API polling and log ingestion to maintain real-time security monitoring. Network-based monitoring techniques, such as packet capture and NetFlow analysis, provide additional visibility into network traffic patterns. By aggregating network flow data alongside security logs, SIEM solutions enhance threat detection capabilities by identifying unusual communication patterns, unauthorized data transfers, and command-and-control (C2) traffic.

Log normalization is a critical step in the aggregation process, ensuring that logs from different sources adhere to a standardized format. Security logs are often generated in different formats, making it challenging to correlate security events across multiple data sources. SIEM solutions use log normalization techniques to standardize log structures, extract key attributes, and categorize security events based on predefined taxonomies. Normalization enables security analysts to search, filter, and analyze security logs efficiently, improving the accuracy of threat detection and forensic investigations. Organizations must define normalization rules that align with industry standards, such as the Common Event Format (CEF) and the Open Security Event

Metadata (OSEM) framework, to ensure consistency across log sources.

Efficient log storage and retention policies are essential for managing large volumes of aggregated security data. Organizations must balance real-time analysis performance with long-term log retention requirements. SIEM solutions implement tiered storage architectures that store frequently accessed logs on high-performance storage while archiving older logs in cost-effective storage solutions. Log retention policies must comply with regulatory requirements, ensuring that security logs are stored for mandated timeframes while minimizing storage costs. Security teams should periodically review log retention policies to ensure compliance with industry regulations and optimize storage utilization.

Data sources and log aggregation form the foundation of an effective SIEM system, providing security teams with the visibility needed to detect, analyze, and respond to threats. By integrating logs from network devices, endpoint security tools, cloud services, authentication systems, and applications, SIEM solutions create a comprehensive security monitoring framework. Organizations must implement robust log collection, normalization, and storage strategies to ensure that their SIEM system operates efficiently and delivers accurate threat intelligence. Properly aggregating and managing security logs enables organizations to detect cyber threats in real time, conduct forensic investigations, and maintain compliance with regulatory requirements.

Integrating SIEM with Other Security Tools

A Security Information and Event Management (SIEM) system is most effective when integrated with other security tools to create a unified and comprehensive security infrastructure. Organizations deploy a variety of cybersecurity solutions, including firewalls, intrusion detection and prevention systems (IDS/IPS), endpoint protection platforms, identity and access management (IAM) systems, cloud security tools, and threat intelligence platforms. Each of these security solutions generates valuable security data that, when integrated with a SIEM system, enhances threat detection, improves incident response, and streamlines security operations. The ability to correlate security events across multiple tools provides security teams with greater visibility and context, enabling them to detect sophisticated attack patterns and respond to threats more effectively.

Firewalls are one of the most critical security tools to integrate with a SIEM system. Firewalls generate logs related to inbound and outbound network traffic, access control rules, and blocked connections. By ingesting firewall logs, a SIEM system can detect anomalies such as repeated access attempts from suspicious IP addresses, unauthorized port scanning, and data exfiltration attempts. When firewall logs are correlated with endpoint security events and user authentication data, security teams can determine whether an attack is originating from inside or outside the organization. Integrating firewalls with a SIEM system also allows security teams to automate response actions, such as blocking malicious IP addresses or modifying firewall rules in real time.

Intrusion detection and prevention systems play a vital role in network security by identifying and mitigating potential threats before they compromise an organization's infrastructure. IDS logs contain alerts about suspicious traffic patterns, unauthorized access attempts, and known attack signatures, while IPS logs provide information about traffic that has been actively blocked or mitigated. Integrating IDS/IPS with a SIEM system allows security teams to correlate intrusion detection events with other security data, providing a broader understanding of attack campaigns. For example, if an IDS detects a brute-force login attempt followed by a successful authentication from the same IP address, the SIEM system can correlate this event with user activity logs to determine whether an account has been compromised.

Endpoint security solutions, including antivirus software, endpoint detection and response (EDR) platforms, and host-based intrusion prevention systems (HIPS), generate logs that provide insight into malware infections, unauthorized file modifications, and suspicious process executions. By integrating endpoint security logs with a SIEM system, security teams can detect malware outbreaks, ransomware attacks, and insider threats more effectively. SIEM platforms analyze endpoint security logs alongside network activity, user authentication events, and threat intelligence feeds to identify patterns that may indicate an advanced persistent threat (APT). When an endpoint is flagged as compromised, SIEM integration allows security teams to trigger automated remediation actions, such as isolating the affected device from the network or executing malware removal scripts.

Identity and access management systems provide authentication and authorization logs that are essential for detecting unauthorized access attempts and account takeovers. Integrating IAM solutions, such as Active Directory (AD), single sign-on (SSO) platforms, and multi-factor authentication (MFA) services, with a SIEM system enhances security monitoring by providing a clear picture of user behavior. SIEM platforms analyze login attempts, privilege escalations, and failed authentication events to detect anomalies that may indicate credential compromise or insider threats. If a SIEM system detects multiple failed login attempts from an unusual location, followed by a successful login with administrative privileges, it can generate an alert and trigger an automated response, such as forcing a password reset or requiring additional authentication steps.

Cloud security tools generate critical security data that must be integrated with a SIEM system to monitor cloud-based infrastructure and services effectively. Organizations that rely on cloud environments such as Amazon Web Services (AWS), Microsoft Azure, and Google Cloud Platform (GCP) must collect logs from cloud security monitoring tools, API gateways, and identity management platforms. Cloud security tools provide visibility into user activity, resource configurations, and data access events. When integrated with a SIEM system, these logs help detect misconfigurations, unauthorized access attempts, and data exfiltration from cloud storage services. Security teams can also leverage SIEM dashboards to monitor cloud-specific security events alongside on-premises logs, ensuring a unified security posture across hybrid and multi-cloud environments.

Threat intelligence platforms enhance the capabilities of a SIEM system by providing real-time information about known cyber threats, malicious IP addresses, attack signatures, and indicators of compromise (IOCs). Integrating threat intelligence feeds with a SIEM system enables organizations to correlate internal security events with external threat data, improving the accuracy of threat detection. If a SIEM system detects an outbound connection to a known command-and-control (C2) server associated with malware, it can trigger an alert and automatically block the connection using firewall policies. Threat intelligence integration also allows security teams to prioritize alerts based on the latest cyber threat trends, reducing false positives and focusing on high-risk incidents.

Security orchestration, automation, and response (SOAR) platforms extend the capabilities of a SIEM system by automating incident response actions and streamlining security workflows. SOAR solutions integrate with SIEM platforms to facilitate automated threat containment, incident escalation, and remediation processes. When a SIEM system detects a security incident, it can trigger predefined response actions, such as sending alerts to security analysts, initiating forensic investigations, or executing automated playbooks. For example, if a SIEM system detects an unauthorized login attempt from a suspicious IP address, a SOAR integration can automatically revoke user access, notify the security team, and generate a compliance report.

Vulnerability management tools provide critical information about security weaknesses in an organization's infrastructure. Integrating a vulnerability management system with a SIEM platform allows security teams to correlate security events with known vulnerabilities, prioritizing threats based on risk level. If a SIEM system detects an exploit attempt targeting a vulnerable application, it can correlate the event with vulnerability scan results to determine whether the targeted system is at risk. This integration helps security teams focus on remediating high-risk vulnerabilities that are actively being exploited, reducing the likelihood of a successful cyberattack.

Log management and forensic analysis tools enhance the data retention and investigation capabilities of a SIEM system. While SIEM solutions provide real-time event correlation and monitoring, integrating with dedicated log management tools ensures that security teams have access to long-term security event data for forensic investigations. When a security incident occurs, security analysts can use SIEM-integrated log management platforms to reconstruct attack timelines, identify root causes, and generate compliance reports. Organizations that require extended log retention for regulatory compliance can leverage cloud-based log storage solutions that integrate with SIEM systems for scalable and cost-effective archival storage.

Integrating SIEM with other security tools creates a unified security ecosystem that enhances threat detection, incident response, and compliance monitoring. By aggregating data from firewalls, intrusion detection systems, endpoint security platforms, identity management solutions, cloud security tools, and threat intelligence platforms, SIEM solutions provide security teams with a centralized and contextualized view of security events. Organizations that invest in SIEM integrations benefit from improved threat visibility, automated response capabilities, and a more efficient security operations workflow. A well-integrated SIEM system serves as the central hub of an organization's cybersecurity infrastructure, enabling security teams to detect and mitigate cyber threats with greater speed and accuracy.

Network and Endpoint Security Integration

Integrating network and endpoint security with a Security Information and Event Management (SIEM) system is essential for providing comprehensive threat detection and incident response capabilities. Network security tools monitor traffic patterns, detect intrusions, and enforce access control policies, while endpoint security solutions focus on protecting individual devices, detecting malware, and preventing unauthorized actions. By combining data from both network and endpoint security tools, a SIEM system enables security teams to correlate events, identify attack patterns, and respond to threats in real time. Proper integration of these security layers enhances visibility, improves forensic investigations, and reduces the time required to contain and mitigate security incidents.

Network security tools, including firewalls, intrusion detection and prevention systems (IDS/IPS), secure web gateways, and network access control (NAC) solutions, generate logs that provide insight into network activity. Firewalls log inbound and outbound traffic, blocked connection attempts, and policy violations. When integrated with a SIEM system, firewall logs help security teams identify suspicious behavior, such as repeated access attempts from untrusted IP addresses, traffic to known malicious domains, and unauthorized port scans. By correlating firewall logs with endpoint security data, SIEM solutions can determine whether a detected anomaly is an isolated event or part of a larger attack campaign.

Intrusion detection and prevention systems play a crucial role in network security by identifying malicious traffic patterns and blocking potential attacks before they reach endpoints. IDS solutions analyze network traffic and generate alerts when they detect known attack signatures, while IPS solutions actively block threats based on predefined rules. SIEM integration with IDS/IPS allows security teams to correlate network-based intrusion attempts with endpoint activity, providing a more complete picture of an attack. If an IDS detects an exploit attempt targeting a vulnerable system, the SIEM system can cross-reference this event with endpoint logs to determine whether the attack was successful and whether additional remediation steps are required.

Network access control solutions regulate which devices are allowed to connect to the network based on predefined security policies. NAC systems enforce authentication and authorization requirements, ensuring that only trusted devices gain access to sensitive resources. When integrated with a SIEM system, NAC logs provide valuable data for detecting unauthorized devices, rogue access points, and potential insider threats. If an unauthorized device attempts to connect to the network, the SIEM system can generate an alert, correlate it with endpoint logs, and initiate an automated response, such as isolating the device or requiring additional authentication.

Secure web gateways (SWG) filter internet traffic to prevent users from accessing malicious websites, downloading malware, or transmitting sensitive data to unauthorized destinations. These gateways generate logs that track user web activity, blocked requests, and content filtering actions. SIEM integration with SWG solutions enables security teams to identify potential phishing attempts, data exfiltration, and shadow IT usage. If a user repeatedly attempts to visit a known malicious website, the SIEM system can correlate this behavior with endpoint security alerts to determine whether the user's device has been compromised or if the user is engaging in risky activities.

Endpoint security solutions provide visibility into individual devices, including desktops, laptops, mobile devices, and servers. These solutions include endpoint detection and response (EDR) platforms, antivirus software, and host-based intrusion prevention systems (HIPS). Integrating endpoint security data with a SIEM system allows security teams to detect malware infections, unauthorized file modifications, and suspicious process executions. If an endpoint begins exhibiting signs of compromise, such as executing unknown scripts, accessing unauthorized files, or establishing outbound connections to suspicious domains, the SIEM system can correlate this behavior with network security logs to determine whether the attack originated from the network or was introduced via a phishing attempt or malicious download.

EDR platforms enhance endpoint security by providing continuous monitoring, behavioral analysis, and automated threat hunting capabilities. These solutions detect suspicious activities, such as privilege escalation, persistence mechanisms, and lateral movement attempts. By integrating EDR telemetry with a SIEM system, security teams gain a centralized view of endpoint threats and can correlate them with network-based anomalies. If an endpoint attempts to connect to a restricted server while simultaneously executing suspicious commands, the SIEM system can generate an alert and initiate a response workflow, such as isolating the endpoint, disabling the affected user account, or triggering an incident investigation.

Host-based intrusion prevention systems add another layer of endpoint security by enforcing security policies and detecting unauthorized changes to system configurations. HIPS solutions monitor file integrity, registry modifications, and process execution to detect indicators of compromise. When integrated with a SIEM system, HIPS logs provide valuable forensic data that helps security teams determine how an attacker gained access to an endpoint and what actions were taken after the compromise. By correlating HIPS data with firewall logs and IDS alerts, SIEM systems can uncover multi-stage attack campaigns and prevent further damage.

Automated threat response is a key benefit of integrating network and endpoint security tools with a SIEM system. When a SIEM platform detects a security incident, it can trigger automated response actions, such as blocking a suspicious IP address at the firewall, quarantining a compromised endpoint, or revoking access privileges for a potentially compromised user account. Security orchestration, automation, and response (SOAR) platforms further enhance SIEM integration by providing predefined playbooks that guide security teams through the incident response process. Automating threat mitigation reduces response times and limits the potential impact of cyberattacks.

Forensic investigations and threat hunting are significantly improved through the integration of network and endpoint security data within a SIEM system. Security analysts can reconstruct attack timelines, determine how an attacker gained initial access, and identify additional compromised systems. By analyzing historical network traffic, endpoint activity logs, and security alerts, security teams can uncover hidden threats, detect stealthy malware, and refine security policies to prevent future incidents. SIEM solutions provide centralized search and visualization tools that enable analysts to quickly analyze security data and extract meaningful insights.

Compliance and regulatory requirements often mandate the collection and retention of both network and endpoint security logs. Many industry regulations, such as GDPR, HIPAA, PCI DSS, and SOX, require organizations to monitor access to sensitive data, detect unauthorized modifications, and maintain audit trails for security events. Integrating network and endpoint security tools with a SIEM system simplifies compliance reporting by automating log collection, event correlation, and incident documentation. Security teams can generate compliance reports that demonstrate adherence to security policies, helping organizations avoid regulatory penalties and maintain a strong security posture.

A comprehensive security strategy requires seamless integration between network security and endpoint security within a SIEM system. By aggregating data from firewalls, IDS/IPS, NAC, secure web gateways, EDR, antivirus software, and HIPS, organizations gain deeper visibility into their security environment. The ability to correlate network-based threats with endpoint activities enhances threat detection, accelerates incident response, and improves forensic investigations. Security teams that leverage SIEM integrations can identify sophisticated attack patterns, mitigate risks more effectively, and strengthen overall cybersecurity resilience.

Cloud Security and SIEM Deployment

The rapid adoption of cloud computing has transformed the way organizations manage IT infrastructure, applications, and data. As businesses migrate critical workloads to cloud environments, security challenges have become more complex. Traditional on-premises security models are no longer sufficient to address the dynamic nature of cloud threats, requiring organizations to implement advanced monitoring and threat detection mechanisms. Security Information and Event Management (SIEM) solutions play a crucial role in cloud security by providing real-time visibility into cloud environments, detecting anomalies, and ensuring compliance with regulatory standards. Deploying a SIEM system in the cloud requires careful planning to integrate with cloud-native security controls, optimize log collection, and manage scalability while minimizing operational overhead.

Cloud security introduces unique challenges that differ from traditional on-premises environments. Unlike static data centers, cloud infrastructures are dynamic, with workloads being spun up and decommissioned on demand. This elasticity complicates security monitoring, as traditional SIEM solutions may struggle to track ephemeral cloud resources. Additionally, cloud environments rely on shared responsibility models, meaning that cloud service providers (CSPs) manage underlying infrastructure security while customers are responsible for securing their applications, data, and user access. SIEM solutions must account for this shared responsibility by aggregating logs from both CSP-managed services and customer-deployed workloads to ensure comprehensive security coverage.

A key component of SIEM deployment in the cloud is log collection and aggregation. Cloud platforms such as Amazon Web Services (AWS), Microsoft Azure, and Google Cloud Platform (GCP) generate vast amounts of security event data across different services, including virtual machines, storage systems, network components, and identity management services. SIEM solutions must integrate with cloud-native logging mechanisms to collect security logs efficiently. AWS CloudTrail, for example, provides detailed logs of API activity, including user authentication events, resource modifications, and policy changes. Similarly, Azure Monitor and Google Cloud Logging capture security-related events across cloud resources. By ingesting logs from these services, a SIEM system can monitor cloud activity for unauthorized access attempts, privilege escalations, and data exfiltration attempts.

Cloud identity and access management (IAM) solutions play a crucial role in securing cloud environments. IAM policies define user permissions, control access to sensitive resources, and enforce multi-factor authentication (MFA). SIEM solutions must integrate with IAM logs to detect anomalies in authentication behavior, unauthorized privilege changes, and potential insider threats. If a user account suddenly gains administrative privileges and attempts to modify security policies, the SIEM system can generate an alert for security teams to investigate. By correlating IAM logs with network traffic and endpoint activity, SIEM solutions enhance identity-based threat detection and prevent unauthorized access to cloud resources.

Network security monitoring in the cloud requires visibility into cloud traffic patterns and data flows. Unlike traditional on-premises networks, cloud environments use virtualized networking models where traffic is routed through cloud-based firewalls, VPN gateways, and load balancers. Cloud-native network security tools such as AWS VPC Flow Logs, Azure Network Watcher, and GCP VPC Flow Logs provide insights into network traffic patterns, blocked connections, and suspicious outbound communications. SIEM integration with these tools enables security teams to detect lateral movement, identify anomalous data transfers, and enforce network segmentation policies. If a cloud-hosted virtual machine starts communicating with an external command-and-control (C2) server, the SIEM system can flag the activity as a potential compromise.

Endpoint security in the cloud presents additional challenges, as organizations must protect cloud-hosted virtual machines, containerized applications, and serverless workloads. Traditional endpoint detection and response (EDR) solutions must be adapted for cloud environments to provide continuous monitoring of cloud-based endpoints. SIEM integration with cloud endpoint security solutions enables threat detection by analyzing process execution logs, file access patterns, and unauthorized administrative actions. If a cloud instance begins executing suspicious scripts or downloading unverified binaries, the SIEM system can correlate these activities with external threat intelligence feeds to determine whether the system has been compromised.

Cloud application security is another critical aspect of SIEM deployment, as organizations increasingly rely on software-as-a-service (SaaS) applications for business operations. SIEM solutions must integrate with cloud access security brokers (CASBs) to monitor user activity within SaaS applications and detect unauthorized data access, file sharing, and policy violations. Many cloud service providers offer built-in security analytics tools, such as AWS GuardDuty, Azure Security Center, and Google Security Command Center, which generate security insights that can be fed into a SIEM system. By consolidating cloud application logs, SIEM solutions enable security teams to detect account takeovers, abnormal API calls, and attempts to bypass access controls.

Compliance and regulatory requirements are major drivers for deploying SIEM solutions in the cloud. Many industries require organizations to maintain security logs, conduct forensic investigations, and generate audit reports to demonstrate compliance with standards such as GDPR, HIPAA, PCI DSS, and ISO 27001. Cloud environments introduce complexities in meeting these requirements, as organizations must ensure that logs are collected, encrypted, and stored for mandated retention periods. SIEM solutions help automate compliance monitoring by aggregating security logs, enforcing access control policies, and generating compliance reports. Cloud-native SIEM deployments allow organizations to implement security controls that align with regulatory frameworks while reducing the complexity of manual audits.

Scalability is a key advantage of cloud-based SIEM solutions, enabling organizations to handle increasing log volumes without requiring costly infrastructure upgrades. Cloud SIEM platforms use distributed computing models to process large amounts of security data in real time, providing elastic scaling based on demand. This flexibility is especially beneficial for organizations with fluctuating security monitoring needs, such as those experiencing seasonal traffic spikes or rapid cloud workload expansions. Cloud SIEM solutions also offer pay-as-you-go pricing models, reducing upfront costs while providing scalability benefits.

Automated threat detection and response capabilities further enhance SIEM effectiveness in cloud environments. By integrating SIEM with security orchestration, automation, and response (SOAR) platforms, organizations can automate threat containment actions, such as revoking access credentials, isolating compromised virtual machines, and blocking malicious IP addresses. Cloud-based SIEM solutions leverage artificial intelligence and machine learning to detect behavioral anomalies, reduce false positives, and accelerate incident response. Security teams can configure automated workflows that trigger remediation actions when suspicious activities are detected, reducing response times and minimizing the impact of security breaches.

Organizations must carefully plan SIEM deployments in the cloud to optimize performance, minimize operational costs, and ensure effective security monitoring. Proper configuration of log collection, data retention policies, and event correlation rules is essential for maximizing SIEM efficiency. Security teams must continuously refine detection rules, integrate threat intelligence feeds, and conduct regular security assessments to adapt to evolving cloud threats. By leveraging cloud-native security tools, implementing automated response mechanisms, and maintaining visibility across cloud environments, SIEM solutions provide organizations with a powerful defense against cyber threats in modern cloud infrastructures.

SIEM in Hybrid and Multi-Cloud Environments

As organizations increasingly adopt hybrid and multi-cloud environments, the complexity of security monitoring and threat detection grows exponentially. A hybrid cloud environment combines on-premises infrastructure with cloud-based services, allowing organizations to leverage the benefits of cloud computing while maintaining control over critical data and applications. A multi-cloud environment, on the other hand, involves using multiple cloud service providers, such as Amazon Web Services (AWS), Microsoft Azure, and

Google Cloud Platform (GCP), to distribute workloads across different cloud platforms. While these approaches offer flexibility, scalability, and resilience, they also introduce new security challenges that require an advanced Security Information and Event Management (SIEM) solution capable of aggregating logs, detecting anomalies, and providing unified visibility across disparate environments.

One of the biggest challenges of securing hybrid and multi-cloud environments is maintaining centralized visibility across all infrastructure components. Traditional SIEM solutions were designed primarily for on-premises environments, where security logs were collected from firewalls, intrusion detection systems, endpoints, and application servers within a single network perimeter. In a hybrid or multi-cloud setup, security logs are generated across multiple locations, including data centers, virtual machines, containers, cloud applications, and third-party services. A SIEM solution deployed in such an environment must integrate with cloud-native logging services while also collecting logs from on-premises security tools to create a single pane of glass for security monitoring.

Cloud service providers offer built-in security monitoring tools that generate valuable security logs. AWS CloudTrail logs API activity, providing insights into resource modifications, authentication events, and potential policy violations. Azure Monitor collects security events across Azure-based services, while Google Cloud Logging provides visibility into security incidents within GCP. A SIEM system must integrate with these cloud-native security tools to aggregate security events, correlate threats, and detect anomalies across cloud environments. Without proper integration, security teams may face blind spots, making it difficult to detect lateral movement, privilege escalations, and unauthorized access.

In a hybrid environment, organizations must ensure that their SIEM system is capable of collecting security logs from both on-premises and cloud-based infrastructure. Network firewalls, endpoint protection platforms, identity and access management (IAM) systems, and intrusion detection systems still play a crucial role in securing on-premises resources. SIEM solutions must ingest logs from these legacy security tools while also monitoring cloud workloads, virtualized infrastructure, and software-as-a-service (SaaS) applications. The ability to correlate on-premises security events with cloud security incidents allows organizations to detect advanced persistent threats (APTs) that attempt to move between on-premises and cloud environments.

Multi-cloud environments introduce additional complexity due to variations in security policies, access control mechanisms, and logging formats across different cloud providers. AWS, Azure, and GCP each have their own identity management systems, network security controls, and security monitoring solutions. A SIEM solution must normalize security logs from different cloud providers to ensure consistency in event correlation and analysis. Without proper normalization, security analysts may struggle to interpret security events, leading to delayed response times and potential security gaps. By implementing standardized log formats, such as the Common Event Format (CEF) or JSON-based structured logging, SIEM solutions can unify security data across multi-cloud environments.

Threat detection in hybrid and multi-cloud environments requires advanced correlation techniques to identify suspicious activity across different platforms. A cyberattack may start with an attacker compromising an on-premises endpoint before attempting to access cloud-based applications using stolen credentials. If security logs from on-premises and cloud environments are analyzed in isolation, security teams may miss the connection between these events, allowing the attacker to move undetected. A SIEM solution capable of multi-layered event correlation can link login attempts from an on-premises identity provider with subsequent access attempts to cloud-based applications, flagging potential credential-based attacks.

User and Entity Behavior Analytics (UEBA) enhances SIEM capabilities in hybrid and multi-cloud environments by identifying deviations from normal user activity. Employees and system administrators frequently switch between on-premises and cloud-based applications, making it difficult to differentiate legitimate activity from malicious actions. SIEM solutions that incorporate UEBA analyze user behavior patterns across different platforms, identifying anomalies such as unusual login locations, excessive access requests, and suspicious data transfers. If a user account that normally accesses cloud storage services from a corporate office suddenly begins downloading large volumes of data from an unknown location, the SIEM system can generate an alert for further investigation.

Cloud security posture management (CSPM) plays an essential role in maintaining security compliance in multi-cloud environments. Misconfigurations in cloud services, such as excessive permissions, publicly exposed storage buckets, and weak authentication policies, are a leading cause of cloud security breaches. SIEM solutions must integrate with CSPM tools to monitor cloud configurations and detect compliance violations in real time. By correlating CSPM alerts with security events from cloud logs, SIEM systems provide security teams with actionable insights to remediate misconfigurations before they are exploited by attackers.

Compliance monitoring is another critical function of SIEM solutions in hybrid and multi-cloud environments. Organizations operating in regulated industries must adhere to standards such as GDPR, HIPAA, PCI DSS, and ISO 27001, which require continuous security monitoring, log retention, and audit reporting. A SIEM solution deployed in a hybrid or multi-cloud setup must be capable of generating compliance reports that consolidate security events across all platforms. Automating compliance monitoring reduces the burden on security teams while ensuring that regulatory requirements are met.

Incident response in hybrid and multi-cloud environments requires seamless integration between SIEM and Security Orchestration, Automation, and Response (SOAR) platforms. When a SIEM system detects a security incident, it must trigger automated response actions that apply across both on-premises and cloud-based infrastructure. For example, if an attacker compromises a cloud-based virtual machine, the SIEM system can initiate an automated response that isolates the affected machine, revokes compromised credentials, and blocks associated IP addresses at the firewall level. By integrating SIEM with SOAR solutions, organizations can streamline incident response workflows and reduce the time needed to mitigate security threats.

Scalability is a major consideration for SIEM deployments in hybrid and multi-cloud environments. Cloud-based SIEM solutions leverage distributed computing and big data analytics to process massive amounts of security events in real time. Organizations must ensure that their SIEM system can dynamically scale based on the volume of security logs generated across on-premises and cloud environments. Elastic scalability ensures that the SIEM system remains responsive during peak usage periods, such as security audits, incident investigations, and large-scale security events.

Deploying a SIEM solution in hybrid and multi-cloud environments requires careful planning, integration, and continuous optimization. Security teams must ensure that security logs from on-premises data centers, cloud platforms, and SaaS applications are collected, correlated, and analyzed in a centralized SIEM system. By leveraging advanced threat detection techniques, behavioral analytics, compliance automation, and automated incident response, SIEM solutions provide organizations with the visibility and security intelligence needed to protect hybrid and multi-cloud infrastructures. Security teams that effectively integrate SIEM across multiple platforms can proactively detect cyber threats, enforce security policies, and maintain compliance in an increasingly complex IT landscape.

Challenges in SIEM Implementation

Deploying a Security Information and Event Management (SIEM) system is a complex process that involves multiple technical, operational, and strategic challenges. While SIEM solutions provide significant benefits in security monitoring, threat detection, and compliance management, organizations often encounter difficulties during implementation. These challenges can stem from factors such as data overload, integration complexity, false positives, performance bottlenecks, and resource constraints. Overcoming these obstacles requires careful planning, continuous optimization, and alignment with the organization's security objectives. Understanding the common challenges in SIEM implementation allows security teams to anticipate potential issues and take proactive measures to enhance the effectiveness of their deployment.

One of the most significant challenges in SIEM implementation is handling the vast volume of security logs generated by modern IT environments. Organizations produce massive amounts of log data from firewalls, intrusion detection systems, endpoint protection tools, cloud services, and business applications. The sheer volume of data can overwhelm a SIEM system, leading to performance degradation, delayed event correlation, and difficulty in identifying meaningful security insights. Organizations must carefully design their SIEM architecture to handle log ingestion efficiently while implementing log filtering, aggregation, and prioritization techniques to focus on the most relevant security events. Without proper log management strategies, SIEM deployments can become slow, unresponsive, and ineffective in detecting threats.

Another major challenge is integrating SIEM with existing security tools and IT infrastructure. Organizations use a variety of security solutions, including firewalls, antivirus platforms, identity and access management (IAM) systems, cloud security tools, and network monitoring solutions. Each of these systems generates security logs in different formats and requires different integration methods. Some legacy security tools may not support standardized log formats or API-based integrations, making it difficult to ensure seamless data ingestion. SIEM solutions must support a wide range of log sources and provide normalization capabilities to convert disparate log formats into a unified structure for efficient analysis. Failure to achieve proper integration limits the visibility of the SIEM system, creating blind spots in security monitoring.

False positives and alert fatigue are common issues in SIEM implementation. SIEM solutions generate alerts based on predefined correlation rules, behavioral analytics, and threat intelligence feeds. However, if the correlation rules are not properly configured, the SIEM system may produce excessive false positives, overwhelming security analysts with irrelevant alerts. When analysts receive too many alerts, they may struggle to differentiate between real threats and benign activities, leading to alert fatigue and potential oversight of critical security incidents. Organizations must fine-tune SIEM alerting mechanisms by adjusting correlation rules, implementing risk-based alert scoring, and leveraging machine learning-based anomaly detection to reduce false positives. Regular rule optimization and continuous monitoring of alert effectiveness help improve SIEM accuracy over time.

Performance optimization is another significant challenge in SIEM implementation. Processing large amounts of security event data in real time requires substantial computational resources, efficient storage mechanisms, and optimized indexing for fast query performance. Organizations that deploy SIEM solutions without adequate infrastructure planning may experience slow query response times, delayed alerting, and system crashes during high data ingestion periods. SIEM performance bottlenecks can impact the effectiveness of security monitoring and delay incident response efforts. Organizations must ensure that their SIEM deployment includes scalable storage solutions, distributed processing capabilities, and performance tuning strategies to maintain real-time threat detection without system slowdowns.

Incident response integration is often a challenge when implementing SIEM solutions. While SIEM systems provide security alerts and correlation analysis, they must be integrated with Security Orchestration, Automation, and Response (SOAR) platforms, ticketing systems, and IT workflows to enable effective incident response. Many organizations struggle to bridge the gap between SIEM alerts and actionable response workflows, resulting in delays in investigating and mitigating security incidents. Automating response actions, such as isolating compromised endpoints, blocking malicious IP addresses, and enforcing access controls, requires careful planning and coordination between security teams and IT operations. Without proper integration, SIEM alerts may remain unaddressed, reducing the overall effectiveness of the security monitoring program.

Scalability is another key challenge in SIEM implementation, particularly for organizations with growing IT infrastructures, multi-cloud deployments, and geographically distributed environments. As an organization's IT footprint expands, the volume of security logs increases, requiring the SIEM system to scale dynamically. Traditional on-premises SIEM solutions often struggle with scalability due to hardware limitations, leading organizations to adopt cloud-based SIEM solutions. While cloud SIEM platforms offer elastic scalability, organizations must ensure that cloud-based log ingestion, storage, and analytics remain cost-effective. Choosing the right SIEM deployment model—on-premises, cloud, or hybrid—is essential for maintaining scalability while balancing performance and cost considerations.

Compliance and regulatory challenges also play a significant role in SIEM implementation. Many organizations must adhere to industry-specific regulations such as GDPR, HIPAA, PCI DSS, and SOX, which require security event monitoring, log retention, and audit reporting. SIEM solutions must be configured to meet regulatory requirements by enforcing data retention policies, enabling access control mechanisms, and generating compliance reports. However, regulatory requirements vary across industries and regions, making it difficult to design a one-size-fits-all SIEM configuration. Organizations must work closely with compliance teams to ensure that their SIEM deployment aligns with legal and industry mandates while avoiding unnecessary storage costs associated with long-term log retention.

Managing and maintaining a SIEM system requires specialized expertise, which can be a challenge for organizations with limited cybersecurity resources. SIEM solutions require continuous monitoring, fine-tuning, and updates to remain effective against evolving cyber threats. Security teams must regularly refine correlation rules, integrate new threat intelligence feeds, and update detection logic to adapt to emerging attack techniques. Organizations that lack in-house SIEM expertise may struggle with proper system configuration, leading to inefficient threat detection and response. Many businesses address this challenge by outsourcing SIEM management to Managed Security Service Providers (MSSPs) or adopting Managed Detection and Response (MDR) services to supplement their internal security operations.

Cost considerations can also present obstacles in SIEM implementation. Traditional SIEM solutions often have high upfront licensing costs, ongoing maintenance fees, and storage expenses associated with long-term log retention. Cloud-based SIEM solutions offer flexible pricing models, but organizations must carefully evaluate costs associated with data ingestion, storage, and analysis to avoid budget overruns. Cost-effective SIEM deployment requires strategic planning to balance security requirements, performance needs, and budget constraints. Optimizing log collection, reducing unnecessary data storage, and prioritizing high-value security events help organizations control SIEM-related expenses without sacrificing security visibility.

Implementing a SIEM solution is a complex process that requires addressing challenges related to data volume, integration complexity, false positives, performance, scalability, incident response, compliance, expertise, and cost management. Organizations must take a structured approach to SIEM deployment by defining security objectives, optimizing log collection, fine-tuning alerting mechanisms, and ensuring seamless integration with existing security tools. By proactively addressing these challenges, organizations can maximize the value of their SIEM investment, enhance their threat detection capabilities, and build a more resilient security posture.

SIEM Data Storage and Retention Policies

Effective data storage and retention policies are essential components of a Security Information and Event Management (SIEM) system. SIEM solutions collect and store vast amounts of security event data from various sources, including network devices, firewalls, intrusion detection systems, cloud services, endpoints, and business applications. These logs serve multiple purposes, such as real-time threat detection, forensic investigations, regulatory compliance, and security trend analysis. However, managing SIEM data storage efficiently requires balancing performance, cost, and compliance requirements while ensuring that security teams can quickly access relevant data when needed. Properly defining storage and retention policies ensures that SIEM deployments remain scalable, cost-effective, and capable of supporting both short-term and long-term security needs.

The volume of security log data generated by modern IT environments is immense, requiring organizations to implement structured data retention policies to avoid excessive storage costs and performance bottlenecks. The retention period for SIEM logs varies based on business needs, compliance mandates, and the level of risk associated with different types of data. Some logs must be retained for only a few months for operational security monitoring, while others must be stored for years to meet industry regulations and legal requirements. Establishing clear retention policies based on regulatory guidelines, business risk assessments, and security best practices helps organizations manage their SIEM data more efficiently.

Compliance requirements play a significant role in determining SIEM data retention policies. Many regulatory frameworks mandate specific retention periods for security logs to ensure that organizations can conduct audits, investigate security incidents, and demonstrate adherence to security policies. For example, the General Data Protection Regulation (GDPR) requires organizations to retain security logs only for as long as necessary, meaning that companies must define data retention policies based on risk assessments. The Health Insurance Portability and Accountability Act (HIPAA) mandates that healthcare organizations retain audit logs for at least six years to track access to patient data. The Payment Card Industry Data Security Standard (PCI DSS) requires organizations handling credit card transactions to retain security event logs for at least one year, with at least three months of data immediately available for forensic investigations. The Sarbanes-Oxley Act (SOX) enforces strict retention policies for financial data logs to prevent fraudulent activity. Organizations must align their SIEM retention policies with these compliance mandates to avoid legal and financial penalties.

Storage tiering is a key strategy for managing SIEM data efficiently while optimizing costs. Not all security logs require the same level of accessibility, and storing all logs in high-performance storage can quickly become expensive. Many organizations implement a tiered storage approach that categorizes logs based on their importance and frequency of access. Hot storage is used for real-time and recent logs that require immediate analysis, such as logs related to active security threats, critical system events, and recent authentication activities. Warm storage is used for logs that need to be available for compliance reporting and historical analysis but are not accessed as frequently. Cold storage is used for long-term archival data that is only needed for forensic investigations and regulatory audits. Cloud-based storage solutions, such as Amazon S3 Glacier, Azure Blob Storage, and Google Coldline Storage, offer cost-effective options for retaining SIEM logs that do not need to be accessed regularly.

Indexing and search performance are crucial considerations in SIEM data storage and retention policies. Security analysts rely on fast search capabilities to investigate security incidents, track anomalies, and generate compliance reports. If logs are not properly indexed, queries can take an excessive amount of time, delaying threat detection and incident response. SIEM solutions optimize indexing by using structured data formats, time-based partitioning, and metadata tagging to facilitate efficient searching. Organizations must strike a balance between storage optimization and search performance by ensuring that frequently accessed logs are indexed in high-performance databases while older logs are compressed and archived in cost-effective storage solutions.

Log integrity and security are critical aspects of SIEM data retention. Security logs contain sensitive information about user activity, system configurations, authentication attempts, and potential security breaches. If these logs are tampered with or deleted, forensic investigations and compliance audits may be compromised. SIEM solutions must implement data integrity mechanisms such as cryptographic hashing, digital signatures, and access controls to prevent unauthorized modifications to security logs. Implementing write-once, read-many (WORM) storage policies ensures that logs cannot be altered or deleted once they are recorded. Encrypting logs both in transit and at rest adds an additional layer of security, protecting sensitive data from unauthorized access.

Data deduplication and compression techniques help organizations reduce SIEM storage costs while maintaining retention policies. Many security logs contain redundant information, and storing duplicate entries unnecessarily increases storage requirements. Deduplication mechanisms identify and remove duplicate log entries, reducing the overall storage footprint without losing critical security data. Compression algorithms further optimize storage by reducing the size of log files while preserving their integrity and searchability. These techniques allow organizations to retain large volumes of security logs while minimizing infrastructure costs.

Retention policies must also account for incident response and forensic investigation requirements. Security teams must have access to historical logs to reconstruct attack timelines, identify attack vectors, and determine the extent of a breach. Retaining logs for an appropriate duration ensures that security teams can analyze past security incidents and detect long-term attack campaigns. Advanced persistent threats (APTs) and stealthy attackers may remain undetected for months, making long-term log retention a necessity for identifying security trends and detecting hidden threats. Organizations must evaluate their risk profiles and determine how long security logs should be retained to support effective threat hunting and forensic analysis.

Automated log lifecycle management simplifies SIEM data retention by enforcing policies that govern log collection, storage, and deletion. Many SIEM solutions include built-in features that automatically move logs between storage tiers based on predefined retention policies. Security teams can configure automated workflows that archive older logs, delete expired records, and enforce regulatory retention requirements without manual intervention. Automating log lifecycle management ensures compliance, reduces storage overhead, and enhances operational efficiency by eliminating the need for manual data management.

Balancing retention policies with cost considerations is a challenge that organizations must address when deploying a SIEM system. While retaining logs for extended periods improves forensic investigation capabilities and ensures regulatory compliance, excessive log retention can lead to high storage costs and system performance issues. Organizations must assess their security, compliance, and operational requirements to determine optimal retention periods for different log types. Conducting periodic reviews of SIEM retention policies allows organizations to adjust storage strategies based on evolving security threats, regulatory changes, and business needs.

SIEM data storage and retention policies must be carefully designed to ensure efficient log management, regulatory compliance, and long-term security visibility. By implementing tiered storage strategies, optimizing search performance, enforcing log integrity measures, and leveraging automated log lifecycle management, organizations can maximize the effectiveness of their SIEM deployments. Well-structured retention policies help security teams respond to threats, conduct forensic investigations, and maintain compliance while minimizing storage costs and operational complexity. Properly managing SIEM data retention ensures that organizations can detect, analyze, and mitigate cyber threats effectively while meeting industry security standards.

Performance Optimization for SIEM Systems

Optimizing the performance of a Security Information and Event Management (SIEM) system is essential for ensuring efficient security monitoring, rapid threat detection, and effective incident response. SIEM solutions process vast amounts of security event data from diverse sources, including network devices, endpoint security tools, cloud environments, and application logs. Without proper optimization, SIEM systems can become overwhelmed by data ingestion, leading to slow query performance, delayed alerts, and an increased risk of missing critical security incidents. Organizations must implement performance optimization strategies to ensure their SIEM system operates smoothly while maintaining scalability, accuracy, and reliability.

One of the primary factors affecting SIEM performance is log ingestion and processing speed. A SIEM system must handle a continuous stream of security logs in real time, processing thousands or even millions of events per second. If the ingestion pipeline is not optimized, log collection delays can lead to gaps in security visibility, affecting the ability to detect threats promptly. Organizations should prioritize efficient log collection methods, including agent-based ingestion, syslog forwarding, and API integrations. Properly configuring log sources to filter out unnecessary data reduces the volume of ingested logs, preventing resource exhaustion and optimizing processing efficiency.

Data normalization and parsing play a crucial role in SIEM performance. Security logs from different sources are often generated in various formats, making it necessary to standardize data structures for effective correlation and analysis. SIEM solutions apply normalization rules to convert raw logs into structured data formats, extracting key attributes such as event type, timestamps, user identities, and source IP addresses. Poorly optimized normalization processes can slow down log processing, increasing query latency and delaying alert generation. Organizations must refine log parsing configurations, eliminate redundant data fields, and use efficient indexing strategies to improve SIEM performance.

Correlation engine efficiency is another critical aspect of SIEM performance optimization. SIEM systems use correlation rules to identify patterns, link related security events, and generate alerts based on predefined detection logic. Overly complex or inefficient correlation rules can consume excessive computing resources, resulting in slow event processing and delayed alerting. Security teams should periodically review and refine correlation rules, removing redundant logic, optimizing conditional expressions, and leveraging machine learning-based anomaly detection for more adaptive threat analysis. Implementing tiered correlation mechanisms—where high-priority threats are analyzed first—improves overall system efficiency.

Storage performance has a significant impact on SIEM responsiveness and query execution speed. Organizations must ensure that their SIEM system utilizes high-performance storage solutions to accommodate rapid data retrieval and indexing. Traditional spinning disk storage can introduce latency, making it difficult to execute security searches in real time. Deploying solid-state drives (SSDs), distributed storage architectures, or cloud-based storage solutions with built-in caching mechanisms enhances SIEM performance by reducing data access times. Additionally, implementing tiered storage policies—where frequently accessed logs remain in fast storage while older logs are archived in lower-cost storage—optimizes both performance and cost efficiency.

Indexing and search optimization are essential for enabling security analysts to conduct efficient investigations within a SIEM system. When security incidents occur, analysts must quickly search through logs to identify attack timelines, determine affected assets, and assess the scope of a breach. If SIEM indexing mechanisms are not optimized, search queries may take excessive time to execute, delaying response efforts. Organizations should implement structured indexing techniques, time-based partitioning, and keyword-based filtering to accelerate log searches. Using pre-indexed fields for common search queries further reduces query execution time, allowing analysts to quickly access relevant security data.

Alerting efficiency directly impacts the effectiveness of SIEM-driven security operations. If a SIEM system generates excessive false positives, security analysts may become overwhelmed by irrelevant alerts, leading to alert fatigue and reduced incident response effectiveness. To optimize SIEM alerting, organizations should fine-tune detection thresholds, implement dynamic alert scoring, and apply behavior-based anomaly detection. SIEM platforms that incorporate user and entity behavior analytics (UEBA) can reduce false positives by learning normal activity patterns and flagging only significant deviations. Additionally, integrating SIEM with a Security Orchestration, Automation, and Response (SOAR) platform enables automated alert triage, prioritizing critical threats while filtering out low-risk events.

Scaling SIEM infrastructure is necessary to maintain performance as log volumes grow over time. Organizations must design their SIEM deployment to scale horizontally or vertically based on demand. Horizontal scaling involves distributing processing workloads across multiple servers or cloud instances, allowing the SIEM system to handle increased data ingestion and analysis. Vertical scaling enhances individual server capacity by upgrading processing power, memory, and storage resources. Cloud-based SIEM solutions offer elastic scalability, dynamically adjusting resource allocation to accommodate fluctuating log volumes. Organizations must continuously monitor their SIEM system's resource utilization and adjust scaling strategies accordingly to prevent performance bottlenecks.

Automated log lifecycle management enhances SIEM performance by ensuring that only relevant logs are retained in high-performance storage while older data is archived or deleted based on predefined retention policies. Organizations should configure automated workflows that categorize logs based on access frequency, regulatory requirements, and security value. By archiving logs that are no longer actively needed for security monitoring but must be retained for compliance, organizations reduce storage costs and improve query performance. Implementing data deduplication and compression further optimizes storage efficiency while preserving essential security information.

Security teams must continuously evaluate and optimize SIEM configurations to adapt to evolving security threats and operational needs. Regular performance assessments, including stress testing, query benchmarking, and alert response evaluations, help identify areas for improvement. Organizations should establish performance monitoring dashboards that track key metrics such as event processing rates, query response times, and system resource utilization. Proactively addressing performance degradation issues before they impact security operations ensures that the SIEM system remains reliable and effective.

Integrating SIEM with threat intelligence feeds enhances detection capabilities while optimizing performance by focusing on high-priority threats. Rather than processing all security logs equally, SIEM solutions should prioritize events associated with known indicators of compromise (IOCs), malicious IP addresses, and active attack campaigns. Threat intelligence-based filtering reduces unnecessary processing overhead while improving detection accuracy. Security teams should regularly update and fine-tune threat intelligence sources to ensure that the SIEM system remains aligned with emerging threats and attack techniques.

Performance optimization for SIEM systems requires a multi-faceted approach, addressing log ingestion efficiency, data normalization, correlation rule refinement, storage optimization, search indexing, alert tuning, and system scalability. By implementing best practices in data management, query performance, and automated log lifecycle handling, organizations ensure that their SIEM system remains responsive, scalable, and capable of detecting cyber threats in real time. Security teams that continuously optimize their SIEM infrastructure can maintain a high level of threat visibility while minimizing operational overhead and resource consumption. Properly tuning SIEM performance enhances the ability to detect and respond to security incidents efficiently, safeguarding the organization's digital assets from evolving cyber threats.

Customization and Fine-Tuning Rules

Customization and fine-tuning of rules in a Security Information and Event Management (SIEM) system are essential for improving threat detection accuracy, reducing false positives, and ensuring that security teams receive meaningful alerts. While SIEM solutions come with predefined correlation rules and event detection capabilities, every organization has unique security requirements, network environments, and operational workflows. Default configurations may not be sufficient to detect advanced threats, leading to missed incidents or excessive noise that overwhelms analysts. Tailoring SIEM rules to fit an organization's specific risk landscape allows security teams to focus on high-priority threats, streamline incident response, and optimize system performance.

The foundation of SIEM customization starts with understanding the organization's IT infrastructure, including network topology, security tools, critical assets, user access patterns, and compliance requirements. Security teams must conduct an initial assessment to identify key log sources, define critical use cases, and establish detection priorities. Logs from firewalls, intrusion detection systems, endpoint protection platforms, cloud services, and identity management solutions must be categorized based on their relevance to security monitoring. Identifying which logs contain valuable security intelligence helps organizations filter out redundant data and improve event correlation efficiency.

Fine-tuning SIEM correlation rules is a critical step in optimizing threat detection. Correlation rules define relationships between multiple security events, allowing the SIEM system to identify attack patterns that may not be obvious when analyzing individual logs in isolation. Default correlation rules provided by SIEM vendors often use generic logic that may not align with an organization's specific security risks. Security teams must modify existing rules and create custom rules to detect threats relevant to their industry, regulatory obligations, and internal policies. For example, financial institutions may need specialized rules to detect fraudulent transactions, while healthcare organizations must prioritize rules that protect patient data from unauthorized access.

Reducing false positives is one of the main challenges when customizing SIEM rules. If correlation rules are too broad, they may trigger excessive alerts, leading to alert fatigue among security analysts. Conversely, overly restrictive rules may result in missed threats, leaving the organization vulnerable to cyberattacks. Security teams should continuously refine rule logic by analyzing historical security events, testing rule effectiveness, and adjusting parameters such as time thresholds, event sequences, and anomaly detection criteria.

Using machine learning-based analytics and behavior-based anomaly detection can further enhance rule accuracy by identifying deviations from normal activity rather than relying solely on static rule sets.

Threshold tuning is a key aspect of rule optimization, ensuring that SIEM alerts reflect meaningful security events without generating unnecessary noise. Many correlation rules use predefined thresholds for triggering alerts, such as a certain number of failed login attempts within a specified time window. Organizations must fine-tune these thresholds based on their unique environment, considering factors such as user behavior, network activity levels, and business operations. For example, a high number of failed login attempts within a short period may indicate a brute-force attack, but if the threshold is set too low, it may generate alerts for routine user mistakes. Adjusting thresholds based on baseline activity ensures that alerts remain relevant and actionable.

SIEM customization also involves defining security use cases tailored to the organization's risk profile. Security teams should identify specific attack scenarios they want to detect, such as insider threats, data exfiltration, credential-based attacks, and advanced persistent threats (APTs). Each use case requires a combination of correlation rules, event filters, and response actions that align with the organization's security objectives. For example, a use case for detecting insider threats may involve monitoring unauthorized file access, unusual data transfers, and privilege escalation attempts. By aligning SIEM rules with defined security use cases, organizations can improve their ability to detect real-world threats and respond proactively.

Automation plays a crucial role in fine-tuning SIEM rules by enabling dynamic adjustments based on evolving security trends. Integrating SIEM with threat intelligence feeds allows organizations to update correlation rules in real time based on newly discovered attack techniques, known malicious IP addresses, and emerging vulnerabilities. Automated rule tuning mechanisms can adjust alert sensitivity based on risk levels, reducing manual intervention while maintaining high detection accuracy. Security teams should implement automation strategies that continuously refine rule sets, eliminating outdated rules and incorporating new detection logic to keep pace with the evolving threat landscape.

Testing and validation are essential to ensure that SIEM rules function as expected. Security teams should conduct simulated attack scenarios, also known as red team exercises or penetration testing, to evaluate rule effectiveness. Testing real-world attack techniques, such as phishing-based credential theft, lateral movement within a network, or privilege escalation attempts, helps determine whether SIEM rules generate the appropriate alerts. Analyzing test results allows security teams to refine rule parameters, adjust detection logic, and improve response workflows. Continuous validation ensures that SIEM rules remain relevant and effective in detecting modern cyber threats.

Adaptive learning techniques further enhance SIEM customization by allowing rules to evolve based on historical data and user behavior patterns. Traditional SIEM rules rely on static conditions that must be manually updated as security requirements change. However, SIEM solutions with machine learning capabilities can analyze past security events, detect long-term trends, and recommend adjustments to rule configurations. For example, if a particular user frequently accesses a specific database during off-hours as part of their normal workflow, the SIEM system can adjust alerts to avoid flagging this behavior as suspicious. Adaptive learning helps security teams reduce unnecessary alerts while maintaining a high level of security awareness.

Custom response actions should be defined alongside fine-tuned SIEM rules to improve incident handling efficiency. When a SIEM alert is triggered, predefined response workflows should dictate how security teams investigate, escalate, and mitigate the potential threat. Automated response mechanisms, such as revoking user credentials, blocking IP addresses, or isolating compromised endpoints, can be integrated with SIEM alerts to reduce manual workload and speed up threat containment. Security teams should ensure that response actions align with business priorities, regulatory requirements, and operational constraints to minimize disruption while effectively mitigating risks.

Documentation and continuous improvement are essential components of SIEM rule customization. Organizations should maintain detailed records of customized rules, including descriptions of their purpose, triggering conditions, and historical performance metrics. Regular reviews of SIEM rule effectiveness should be conducted to determine whether adjustments are needed based on emerging threats, operational changes, or compliance updates. Security teams should also collaborate with business stakeholders to ensure that SIEM rules align with broader security policies and risk management strategies. A structured approach to documentation and rule refinement ensures that SIEM configurations remain adaptable and effective in protecting organizational assets.

Customization and fine-tuning of SIEM rules are critical for maximizing threat detection accuracy, reducing alert fatigue, and improving security operations. By refining correlation rules, optimizing thresholds, defining security use cases, leveraging automation, and continuously testing rule effectiveness, organizations can enhance the overall efficiency of their SIEM deployment. Well-structured customization strategies ensure that SIEM solutions remain aligned with the organization's evolving security landscape, providing timely and actionable insights that enable proactive threat mitigation. Security teams that invest in fine-tuning SIEM rules gain a competitive advantage in detecting, analyzing, and responding to cyber threats effectively.

Security Analytics and Machine Learning in SIEM

Security Information and Event Management (SIEM) systems have evolved significantly over the years, incorporating advanced security analytics and machine learning capabilities to enhance threat detection, incident response, and anomaly detection. Traditional SIEM solutions relied heavily on rule-based correlation and predefined detection signatures to identify security threats. While these methods remain valuable, they are often limited in detecting sophisticated cyber threats that evade signature-based detection. Modern SIEM platforms integrate machine learning algorithms and security analytics to provide more adaptive, context-aware, and proactive security monitoring. By leveraging data science techniques, SIEM solutions can identify hidden attack patterns, reduce false positives, and improve the overall efficiency of security operations.

Security analytics in SIEM involves the systematic examination of security event data to detect anomalies, uncover attack trends, and predict potential threats. Unlike traditional SIEM implementations that rely solely on static rules, security analytics applies advanced mathematical models and statistical techniques to analyze vast amounts of security logs in real time. Organizations generate massive volumes of security data from firewalls, network traffic logs, endpoint security tools, cloud services, and identity management systems. Processing this data manually is impractical, making automated security analytics a crucial component of modern SIEM systems. By identifying deviations from normal behavior, security analytics helps detect threats that may otherwise go unnoticed in a rule-based SIEM environment.

Machine learning enhances SIEM capabilities by enabling systems to adapt to new and emerging threats without requiring constant manual rule updates. Machine learning models are designed to recognize patterns in historical security data and apply those insights to detect abnormal behavior. One of the key advantages of machine learning in SIEM is its ability to analyze vast datasets and identify relationships between seemingly unrelated security events. For example, a traditional SIEM system may flag a brute-force login attempt if it detects multiple failed login attempts from the same IP address within a short period. However, a machine learning-based SIEM system can go beyond simple threshold detection by considering additional factors such as geographic location, time of day, user access history, and known attack tactics.

User and Entity Behavior Analytics (UEBA) is a critical application of machine learning in SIEM. UEBA analyzes the behavior of users, devices, and applications to establish a baseline of normal activity. Once normal behavior is established, machine learning models can detect deviations that may indicate a security threat. If an employee who typically logs in from the same geographic location suddenly accesses the network from an unusual location and downloads a large volume of sensitive files, UEBA can flag this as suspicious behavior. Traditional rule-based SIEM systems may not detect this anomaly unless a predefined correlation rule exists for such activity. By leveraging UEBA, SIEM systems can identify insider threats, account takeovers, and compromised credentials with greater accuracy.

Supervised and unsupervised machine learning techniques play a role in enhancing SIEM threat detection capabilities. Supervised learning involves training a machine learning model using labeled datasets, where past security events are categorized as benign or malicious. The model learns from historical attack patterns and applies this knowledge to classify new security events in real time. This approach is useful for detecting known threats, such as malware infections, phishing attempts, and brute-force attacks. Unsupervised learning, on the other hand, does not rely on predefined labels. Instead, it analyzes security data to identify patterns and clusters of activity that deviate from the norm. This technique is particularly effective in detecting zero-day attacks, advanced persistent threats (APTs), and novel attack techniques that do not match existing threat signatures.

Anomaly detection is a core component of machine learning-driven SIEM analytics. By continuously monitoring security event data, anomaly detection algorithms can identify outliers that deviate from established behavioral patterns. These anomalies may indicate potential security incidents such as unauthorized access, privilege escalation, or data exfiltration. Anomaly detection models use various techniques, including statistical analysis, clustering, and neural networks, to detect subtle deviations that might not trigger traditional SIEM correlation rules. For example, if an internal server that usually communicates only with internal systems suddenly establishes connections to an external IP address known for malicious activity, anomaly detection algorithms can flag this event for further investigation.

Threat intelligence integration further enhances machine learning-driven SIEM analytics. By incorporating external threat intelligence feeds, SIEM systems can enrich security event data with real-time information about known malicious IP addresses, attack signatures, and emerging threats. Machine learning models can correlate threat intelligence data with internal security logs to identify potential indicators of compromise (IOCs). If a SIEM system detects an outbound connection to an IP address associated with a known botnet, machine learning algorithms can prioritize this alert based on the threat reputation of the IP address and other contextual factors. This approach helps security analysts focus on high-risk threats while reducing false positives.

Reducing false positives is a significant benefit of machine learning in SIEM. Traditional rule-based SIEM solutions often generate a high volume of alerts, many of which are false positives that do not indicate actual security threats. Security teams may become overwhelmed by excessive alerts, leading to alert fatigue and delayed response times. Machine learning models can analyze past security incidents, learn from analyst feedback, and refine detection algorithms to reduce noise. By prioritizing high-confidence alerts and filtering out benign activity, machine learning-driven SIEM systems improve analyst efficiency and allow security teams to focus on genuine threats.

Predictive analytics is another valuable application of machine learning in SIEM. By analyzing historical security data, machine learning models can predict potential attack trends and proactively identify vulnerabilities. Predictive analytics enables security teams to anticipate attack techniques based on evolving threat landscapes. For example, if an organization experiences repeated phishing attacks targeting specific departments, predictive models can analyze email metadata, employee behavior, and attacker tactics to preemptively strengthen phishing defenses. This proactive approach allows organizations to take preventive security measures before an attack occurs, reducing overall risk exposure.

Automating response actions is a key advantage of integrating machine learning with SIEM. By combining SIEM with Security Orchestration, Automation, and Response (SOAR) platforms, organizations can implement automated threat mitigation workflows. Machine learning models can classify security incidents based on severity and trigger predefined response actions such as blocking malicious IP addresses, disabling compromised user accounts, or isolating infected endpoints. Automated responses reduce the time required to contain security incidents, minimizing potential damage and improving overall security resilience.

Security analytics and machine learning have transformed SIEM capabilities by enabling intelligent threat detection, behavioral analysis, anomaly identification, and predictive modeling. By leveraging advanced analytics techniques, organizations can detect previously unknown threats, reduce false positives, and enhance security operations efficiency. Machine learning-driven SIEM solutions provide a more adaptive and proactive approach to cybersecurity, allowing organizations to respond to threats in real time and improve their overall security posture. As cyber threats continue to evolve, the integration of machine learning into SIEM will play an increasingly vital role in protecting organizations from sophisticated attacks.

Threat Intelligence Feeds and SIEM Integration

Threat intelligence feeds play a crucial role in enhancing the capabilities of a Security Information and Event Management (SIEM) system by providing real-time information about emerging cyber threats, malicious indicators of compromise (IOCs), and attacker tactics, techniques, and procedures (TTPs). By integrating external threat intelligence sources with SIEM, organizations can improve their ability to detect and respond to advanced threats, reduce false positives, and enhance situational awareness. Threat intelligence feeds provide valuable context to security events, enabling security teams to prioritize high-risk alerts and focus on the most pressing security incidents. Effective integration of threat intelligence with SIEM allows organizations to stay ahead of evolving cyber threats and strengthen their overall security posture.

Threat intelligence feeds come from a variety of sources, including commercial vendors, open-source threat intelligence communities, government agencies, and industry-specific Information Sharing and Analysis Centers (ISACs). Commercial threat intelligence providers offer curated, high-confidence threat data that includes known malicious IP addresses, domain names, URLs, hash values of malware samples, and attack campaign details. Open-source threat intelligence feeds, such as AlienVault Open Threat Exchange (OTX), Abuse.ch, and the MITRE ATT&CK framework, provide free and publicly available threat data contributed by the cybersecurity community. Government-backed initiatives like the Cybersecurity and Infrastructure Security Agency (CISA) and Europol's Cybercrime Center also share threat intelligence to help organizations defend against cybercriminal activities. Industry-specific ISACs enable organizations within the same sector to share threat intelligence and collaborate on mitigating targeted attacks.

Integrating threat intelligence feeds with SIEM enhances security event correlation by providing additional context to security logs. Without threat intelligence, SIEM systems rely on predefined correlation rules and anomaly detection techniques to identify suspicious activities. However, these methods may not always detect new or sophisticated threats. By ingesting real-time threat intelligence, a SIEM system can automatically correlate security events with known IOCs, identifying potential compromises more accurately. For example, if a SIEM system detects outbound connections from an internal server to an IP address listed in a threat intelligence feed as associated with a botnet, the system can immediately flag the activity as a high-priority alert.

Automating threat intelligence ingestion is essential for ensuring that SIEM systems remain up to date with the latest threat data. Cyber threats evolve rapidly, and static rule-based detection alone is insufficient for identifying new attack vectors. SIEM solutions must support automated ingestion of threat intelligence feeds using industry-standard formats such as Structured Threat Information eXpression (STIX), Trusted Automated Exchange of Indicator Information (TAXII), and OpenIOC. These formats enable seamless integration between threat intelligence providers and SIEM platforms, ensuring that security teams receive real-time updates on emerging threats. By automating feed ingestion, organizations can reduce the manual effort required to update SIEM detection logic and improve threat detection efficiency.

Prioritizing alerts using threat intelligence feeds helps security analysts distinguish between low-risk and high-risk events. A common challenge in SIEM deployments is the generation of excessive alerts, many of which may be false positives or low-priority incidents. Threat intelligence feeds enable SIEM systems to assign risk scores to security events based on the reputation of involved IP addresses, domains, or file hashes. If an authentication attempt originates from an IP address known to be associated with a recent phishing campaign, the SIEM system can prioritize this event for immediate investigation. Risk-based alert prioritization ensures that security analysts focus on the most critical threats first, reducing alert fatigue and improving response times.

Threat intelligence feeds also enhance SIEM-driven forensic investigations by providing historical context on known cyber threats. When investigating a security incident, analysts can use threat intelligence data to determine whether a detected activity is part of a larger attack campaign. If a compromised endpoint is found to be communicating with a command-and-control (C2) server listed in a historical threat intelligence database, analysts can quickly assess the severity of the breach and take appropriate remediation steps. By integrating historical threat intelligence with SIEM, organizations can improve the accuracy of incident investigations and identify persistent threats that may have gone undetected.

Threat intelligence-driven SIEM automation enables organizations to respond to security incidents more efficiently. By integrating SIEM with Security Orchestration, Automation, and Response (SOAR) platforms, organizations can automate threat mitigation actions based on threat intelligence data. For example, if a SIEM system detects malicious activity originating from a blacklisted IP address, it can automatically trigger a SOAR workflow that blocks the IP address at the firewall, revokes user access privileges, and alerts the security team. Automated threat response reduces the time required to contain security incidents, minimizing the potential impact of cyberattacks.

Customizing threat intelligence feeds for specific organizational needs improves the relevance of threat data ingested by the SIEM system. Not all threat intelligence is equally valuable to every organization. A financial institution may prioritize threat intelligence related to banking trojans and fraud schemes, while a healthcare provider may focus on intelligence related to ransomware attacks targeting patient records. Organizations should configure their SIEM systems to filter threat intelligence feeds based on industry relevance, geographic focus, and operational priorities. By refining threat intelligence ingestion, SIEM systems can generate more meaningful alerts and reduce unnecessary noise.

Enriching SIEM alerts with threat intelligence provides additional context to security analysts, helping them make informed decisions during incident investigations. When an alert is triggered, SIEM systems can automatically query external threat intelligence sources to retrieve information about the associated indicators. If an alert involves a suspicious domain, the SIEM system can pull additional data such as domain registration details, associated malware campaigns, and prior attack reports. Providing analysts with enriched threat intelligence at the time of alert generation enables faster decision-making and improves the accuracy of threat assessments.

Continuous evaluation of threat intelligence effectiveness is necessary to ensure that SIEM integrations remain valuable over time. Threat intelligence feeds must be regularly assessed for accuracy, relevance, and timeliness. If a feed generates an excessive number of false positives or outdated threat indicators, it may need to be refined or replaced with a more reliable source. Organizations should monitor the impact of threat intelligence integration on SIEM performance, adjusting configurations to improve detection efficiency while minimizing resource consumption. Threat intelligence management platforms can assist in aggregating, validating, and optimizing feeds before ingestion into SIEM systems.

Threat intelligence feeds and SIEM integration provide organizations with a proactive approach to cybersecurity by enabling real-time threat detection, automated incident response, and enhanced forensic investigations. By leveraging external threat intelligence sources, SIEM systems can correlate security events with known attack indicators, prioritize high-risk alerts, and reduce response times. Automated threat intelligence ingestion, risk-based alert prioritization, and custom feed configurations improve the efficiency of security operations while minimizing alert fatigue. As cyber threats continue to evolve, integrating threat intelligence with SIEM remains a critical component of modern security strategies, helping organizations defend against sophisticated and emerging cyber threats.

SIEM for Insider Threat Detection

Insider threats pose one of the most significant security risks to organizations, as they originate from employees, contractors, or business partners who already have legitimate access to internal systems and sensitive data. Unlike external cyberattacks, insider threats are more challenging to detect because they do not always involve unauthorized access from unknown sources. Instead, they may manifest as misuse of privileges, data exfiltration, unauthorized modifications, or malicious intent from disgruntled employees. Security Information and Event Management (SIEM) systems play a critical role in identifying and mitigating insider threats by analyzing user behavior, correlating security events, and detecting anomalies that indicate potential security risks. By leveraging advanced analytics, behavioral monitoring, and machine learning capabilities, SIEM solutions can provide early warnings of insider threats and help security teams take proactive measures to prevent data breaches and unauthorized activities.

One of the key advantages of using SIEM for insider threat detection is its ability to aggregate and analyze logs from multiple data sources. Organizations generate vast amounts of security event data from authentication systems, endpoint devices, file servers, email platforms, cloud services, and network traffic logs. By collecting and correlating logs from these sources, SIEM solutions can detect patterns of suspicious activity that may indicate an insider threat. For example, if an employee suddenly accesses a large volume of sensitive files outside of their normal working hours, the SIEM system can generate an alert for further investigation. By continuously monitoring user activity across various systems, SIEM solutions provide comprehensive visibility into potential insider threats.

User and Entity Behavior Analytics (UEBA) is a critical component of insider threat detection within a SIEM system. Traditional security monitoring relies on predefined rules and signature-based detection, which may not be effective against insiders who misuse their privileges in subtle ways. UEBA enhances SIEM capabilities by establishing baselines of normal user behavior and identifying deviations that may indicate malicious intent. If an employee who typically logs in from a corporate office suddenly begins accessing company systems from an unusual geographic location, UEBA can flag this as an anomaly. Similarly, if a user downloads an unusually large amount of confidential data compared to their normal activity, SIEM can trigger an alert for security teams to investigate. By focusing on behavioral deviations rather than predefined attack signatures, SIEM with UEBA improves the detection of insider threats that would otherwise go unnoticed.

Privileged access monitoring is another essential aspect of insider threat detection. Employees with elevated privileges, such as system administrators, database managers, and IT security personnel, have greater access to critical systems and sensitive data. If a privileged user misuses their access to modify security configurations, delete logs, or access restricted information, it can lead to serious security incidents. SIEM solutions help monitor privileged user activity by tracking logins, system changes, and access to sensitive resources. If an administrator grants themselves additional privileges or modifies security policies without proper authorization, the SIEM system can generate an alert for review. Organizations can further strengthen insider threat detection by implementing just-in-time privilege escalation, where users are granted elevated access only when needed and for a limited duration.

Data exfiltration is a major concern in insider threat scenarios, as malicious insiders may attempt to steal sensitive company information for personal gain, competitive advantage, or corporate espionage. SIEM solutions help detect data exfiltration by monitoring file transfers, email attachments, and cloud storage access. If an employee who typically accesses a limited set of documents suddenly starts transferring large amounts of data to external USB devices, personal email accounts, or unauthorized cloud storage, SIEM can identify this behavior as suspicious. By integrating with Data Loss Prevention (DLP) solutions, SIEM systems can enforce security policies that block unauthorized data transfers and prevent sensitive information from leaving the organization.

SIEM solutions also play a crucial role in detecting unauthorized access attempts and account misuse. Insider threats may involve employees attempting to access systems or files beyond their authorized permissions. SIEM can monitor failed login attempts, access control policy violations, and lateral movement within the network to identify suspicious behavior. If an employee repeatedly attempts to access restricted systems or uses credentials belonging to another user, the SIEM system can flag the activity for investigation. By integrating with Identity and Access Management (IAM) solutions, SIEM can correlate authentication events with user roles and permissions, ensuring that only authorized personnel access critical resources.

Email monitoring and communication analysis are valuable components of SIEM-based insider threat detection. Employees may attempt to share confidential information through corporate or personal email accounts, chat applications, or collaboration platforms. SIEM solutions can integrate with email security tools to analyze email content, detect suspicious attachments, and flag emails containing sensitive keywords. If an employee frequently communicates with external contacts using encrypted file attachments, SIEM can generate an alert for further investigation. By correlating email activity with other security events, such as unusual login locations or unauthorized file access, SIEM enhances insider threat detection capabilities.

Automated incident response is an essential feature of modern SIEM solutions that helps mitigate insider threats quickly. When SIEM detects a potential insider threat, it can trigger predefined response actions, such as revoking user access, isolating compromised devices, or notifying security teams for further investigation. By integrating with Security Orchestration, Automation, and Response (SOAR) platforms, SIEM solutions can streamline incident response workflows, reducing the time required to contain security incidents. Automated responses help organizations minimize the impact of insider threats while allowing security analysts to focus on investigating complex cases.

Compliance and audit reporting are additional benefits of using SIEM for insider threat detection. Many industry regulations, such as GDPR, HIPAA, PCI DSS, and SOX, require organizations to monitor user activity, enforce access controls, and maintain audit logs of security events. SIEM solutions provide built-in compliance reporting tools that enable organizations to demonstrate adherence to regulatory requirements. If an insider threat incident occurs, SIEM logs serve as valuable forensic evidence for determining the scope of the breach and identifying the responsible parties. By maintaining comprehensive audit trails, organizations can ensure accountability and strengthen security governance.

Continuous improvement and fine-tuning of SIEM rules are necessary to enhance insider threat detection over time. Security teams should regularly review SIEM alerts, analyze false positives, and refine detection rules based on evolving insider threat tactics. Conducting red team exercises, where ethical hackers simulate insider threat scenarios, can help organizations assess the effectiveness of their SIEM detection capabilities. By incorporating threat intelligence and behavior-based analytics, SIEM solutions can adapt to new attack techniques and provide more accurate threat detection.

SIEM systems offer a powerful defense against insider threats by monitoring user behavior, detecting unauthorized access attempts, identifying data exfiltration, and enforcing security policies. By integrating UEBA, privileged access monitoring, automated response actions, and compliance reporting, SIEM solutions provide a comprehensive approach to mitigating insider risks. Organizations that leverage SIEM for insider threat detection can proactively identify and respond to security incidents, protecting their critical assets from both malicious and negligent insider activities.

Automating Incident Response with SIEM

Security Information and Event Management (SIEM) systems play a critical role in modern cybersecurity by providing real-time monitoring, threat detection, and incident response capabilities. As organizations face an increasing number of security threats, manually investigating and responding to every alert becomes impractical. Security teams are often overwhelmed by the sheer volume of alerts generated by SIEM systems, leading to delayed responses and, in some cases, missed critical incidents. Automating incident response with SIEM enhances efficiency by reducing the manual workload, improving response times, and ensuring that security threats are contained before they escalate. By integrating automation into SIEM workflows, organizations can streamline security operations, minimize human error, and improve overall cybersecurity resilience.

Automated incident response in SIEM relies on predefined rules, machine learning algorithms, and orchestration platforms to take immediate action when a security event is detected. When an SIEM system identifies an anomaly or a confirmed security incident, it can trigger automated workflows that initiate mitigation steps, notify security personnel, and document the response process. Automation reduces the time between detection and remediation, ensuring that security threats are neutralized before they cause significant damage.

Organizations that implement SIEM automation can achieve a more proactive security posture by responding to threats in real time instead of relying on manual intervention.

One of the key benefits of automating incident response with SIEM is the ability to contain threats before they spread. Cyberattacks often progress in multiple stages, starting with an initial compromise, followed by lateral movement, privilege escalation, and data exfiltration. If an attacker gains access to an organization's network, a slow response could allow them to move deeper into critical systems. SIEM automation can detect early indicators of compromise and take immediate action to contain the threat. For example, if SIEM detects a brute-force login attempt followed by successful unauthorized access, it can trigger an automated workflow that disables the compromised account, blocks the attacker's IP address, and alerts the security team for further investigation.

Automated response actions in SIEM can be customized based on the severity of the detected threat. Low-risk incidents, such as an employee using a weak password, may trigger an automatic email notification requesting a password reset. Medium-risk events, such as unauthorized file access, could result in temporary access restrictions while security analysts investigate further. High-risk incidents, such as malware infections or ransomware activity, may trigger immediate actions such as isolating infected endpoints, blocking network traffic, and revoking compromised credentials. By categorizing threats based on risk level, SIEM automation ensures that the appropriate response is applied based on the severity of the incident.

Integration with Security Orchestration, Automation, and Response (SOAR) platforms enhances SIEM automation by providing centralized incident response management. SOAR platforms work alongside SIEM solutions to coordinate automated response workflows, orchestrate actions across multiple security tools, and facilitate communication between security teams. When SIEM detects a security event, it can pass the incident details to a SOAR platform, which then executes predefined playbooks that automate the response. Playbooks define the sequence of actions to take when a specific type of incident occurs, ensuring a consistent and repeatable response process. For example, a phishing attack playbook may include steps such as quarantining the malicious email, notifying affected users, scanning impacted endpoints, and updating email filtering rules to block similar threats.

Machine learning and artificial intelligence (AI) further enhance SIEM automation by improving threat detection accuracy and reducing false positives. Traditional SIEM systems rely on static correlation rules, which require continuous updates to remain effective. However, machine learning algorithms can analyze historical security data, identify patterns of normal behavior, and detect deviations that may indicate potential threats. By integrating AI-driven analytics, SIEM automation can prioritize high-risk threats while filtering out low-priority alerts. This reduces the burden on security analysts, allowing them to focus on investigating real security incidents rather than sorting through large volumes of false positives.

Automated threat intelligence enrichment is another key feature of SIEM automation. SIEM systems can integrate with external threat intelligence feeds to gather real-time information on known malicious IP addresses, domains, file hashes, and attack signatures. When a SIEM system detects a suspicious activity, it can automatically query threat intelligence databases to determine if the detected indicators are associated with known cyber threats. If a detected IP address is linked to a botnet or a command-and-control (C2) server, SIEM can automatically block the connection, preventing further communication with the attacker. Automating threat intelligence enrichment enhances incident response by providing additional context to security alerts, improving the accuracy of threat classification and reducing manual investigation time.

Incident response automation also plays a crucial role in compliance and regulatory requirements. Many industry regulations, such as GDPR, HIPAA, PCI DSS, and NIST, require organizations to implement incident response plans, maintain audit logs, and ensure timely reporting of security breaches. SIEM automation helps organizations meet these compliance requirements by automatically documenting security incidents, generating reports, and ensuring that response actions are executed in accordance with predefined security policies. Automated workflows ensure that incidents are handled consistently, reducing the risk of non-compliance and improving overall security governance.

Automated forensic analysis capabilities in SIEM allow security teams to investigate security incidents more efficiently. When an incident is detected, SIEM automation can collect relevant security logs, correlate related events, and generate an incident timeline. This accelerates the forensic investigation process, enabling analysts to determine the root cause of the attack, identify affected systems, and take corrective actions. If an attacker attempts to move laterally within the network, SIEM automation can track their activity across multiple systems, helping security teams contain the attack before further damage occurs.

Organizations must carefully design and fine-tune their SIEM automation strategies to ensure that automated responses do not disrupt normal business operations. Overly aggressive automation policies may result in false alarms, unnecessary account lockouts, or unintended system outages. Security teams should conduct regular testing of automated workflows, review incident response playbooks, and continuously refine detection rules to improve accuracy. A balanced approach to automation ensures that SIEM systems effectively contain threats without negatively impacting legitimate user activities.

Implementing automation in SIEM requires a strategic approach that aligns with organizational security policies, risk management frameworks, and business objectives. Security teams should start by identifying key security use cases where automation can provide the most value, such as phishing response, malware containment, insider threat detection, and compliance reporting. Gradually expanding automation capabilities based on real-world threat scenarios ensures a smooth transition from manual to automated incident response. Continuous monitoring and optimization of automated workflows help organizations maintain an adaptive and efficient security posture.

Automating incident response with SIEM significantly enhances an organization's ability to detect, analyze, and mitigate security threats in real time. By integrating AI-driven analytics, SOAR platforms, threat intelligence feeds, and automated forensic analysis, SIEM automation reduces response times, minimizes manual workload, and improves overall security effectiveness. A well-implemented SIEM automation strategy ensures that security teams can respond to threats faster, contain attacks before they escalate, and maintain compliance with industry regulations. As cyber threats continue to evolve, SIEM automation remains a crucial element in modern security operations, enabling organizations to proactively defend against sophisticated attacks while optimizing security resources.

Security Orchestration, Automation, and Response (SOAR)

Security Orchestration, Automation, and Response (SOAR) is a critical component of modern cybersecurity operations, enabling organizations to improve efficiency, reduce response times, and manage security incidents more effectively. As cyber threats grow in volume and complexity, security teams face the challenge of handling an overwhelming number of alerts while ensuring that real threats are quickly identified and mitigated. SOAR solutions enhance security operations by integrating multiple security tools, automating repetitive tasks, and orchestrating incident response workflows. By leveraging SOAR, organizations can streamline security processes, reduce human error, and improve the overall effectiveness of their security posture.

SOAR platforms are designed to centralize security event data, enabling security teams to manage incidents from a unified interface. Traditional security operations centers (SOCs) often rely on multiple tools for threat detection, log analysis, vulnerability management, and incident response. This fragmented approach can lead to inefficiencies, as analysts must switch between different systems to investigate security incidents. SOAR solutions integrate with Security Information and Event Management (SIEM) systems, endpoint detection and response (EDR) tools, firewall logs, threat intelligence feeds, and other security technologies to create a cohesive security ecosystem. By consolidating security data and automating response actions, SOAR platforms allow analysts to work more efficiently and focus on high-priority threats.

Automation is one of the core functions of SOAR, allowing security teams to execute predefined response actions without manual intervention. Many security incidents, such as phishing attempts, brute-force login attempts, and malware infections, follow predictable patterns that can be addressed through automated workflows. When a security event is detected, SOAR can trigger automated actions such as blocking malicious IP addresses, isolating compromised endpoints, disabling suspicious user accounts, or generating detailed reports for further investigation. By automating repetitive tasks, SOAR reduces the burden on security analysts, enabling them to focus on complex threat investigations rather than routine administrative work.

Playbooks are an essential feature of SOAR platforms, defining the sequence of actions that should be taken in response to specific security incidents. A playbook is a structured workflow that outlines the steps to analyze, contain, and remediate a security threat. For example, a phishing response playbook may include automated email scanning, URL reputation checks, quarantining malicious messages, and notifying affected users. Similarly, a ransomware response playbook may involve isolating infected machines, blocking communication with known command-and-control servers, and restoring files from backups. SOAR playbooks ensure consistency in incident response, allowing organizations to enforce security policies and minimize the impact of security breaches.

Threat intelligence integration is another critical aspect of SOAR, enabling organizations to enhance detection capabilities by leveraging external threat intelligence feeds. Cyber threats evolve rapidly, and security teams must continuously update their detection and response mechanisms to stay ahead of attackers. SOAR platforms can ingest threat intelligence from commercial providers, open-source feeds, and industry-specific Information Sharing and Analysis Centers (ISACs). When an alert is generated, SOAR can automatically enrich the security event with contextual information from threat intelligence databases, helping analysts determine whether an alert represents a genuine threat. By automating threat intelligence correlation, SOAR reduces investigation time and improves threat-hunting efficiency.

Incident response coordination is a major benefit of SOAR, particularly for large organizations with distributed security teams. When a security incident occurs, multiple stakeholders—including IT teams, legal departments, and compliance officers—may need to be involved in the response process. SOAR platforms facilitate collaboration by providing a centralized platform where security analysts can share findings, assign tasks, and document incident response actions. Automated case management ensures that incidents are tracked from detection to resolution, maintaining a clear audit trail of all response activities. This structured approach to incident management improves accountability and ensures that security incidents are handled efficiently.

SOAR also enhances compliance and regulatory reporting by automating the collection of security event data and generating detailed reports. Many industries are subject to strict security regulations, such as GDPR, HIPAA, PCI DSS, and NIST, which require organizations to maintain logs, conduct security audits, and demonstrate compliance with security policies. SOAR solutions simplify compliance management by automating log retention, generating incident response reports, and ensuring that security teams follow standardized procedures. Automated compliance reporting reduces the administrative burden on security teams while ensuring that organizations meet regulatory requirements.

Adaptive learning capabilities in SOAR platforms improve incident response effectiveness by analyzing past security incidents and recommending optimizations to security workflows. Machine learning algorithms can assess historical threat data, identify common attack patterns, and suggest refinements to playbooks based on previous incidents. For example, if an organization repeatedly encounters a specific type of malware attack, SOAR can recommend adjustments to firewall policies, endpoint security configurations, and automated remediation steps. This continuous improvement process ensures that security operations evolve over time, becoming more resilient against emerging threats.

One of the challenges organizations face when implementing SOAR is ensuring seamless integration with existing security tools and workflows. Security environments vary widely across organizations, and SOAR platforms must be configured to work with different SIEM solutions, intrusion detection systems, cloud security tools, and access management platforms. Custom API integrations and standardized data formats such as STIX and TAXII enable SOAR solutions to interact with a broad range of security technologies. Organizations must carefully plan their SOAR deployment to ensure that automated workflows align with their security policies and operational requirements.

Scalability is another important factor to consider when implementing SOAR. As organizations grow, the volume of security alerts and incidents increases, requiring scalable automation to handle a larger workload. Cloud-based SOAR solutions provide on-demand scalability, allowing organizations to expand their automation capabilities without significant infrastructure investment. By leveraging cloud-native SOAR platforms, security teams can manage large-scale security operations efficiently while maintaining flexibility in their response strategies.

Human oversight remains a critical component of SOAR implementation. While automation significantly improves response speed and efficiency, security teams must ensure that automated actions do not disrupt legitimate business activities. False positives can occur, and automated responses must be carefully fine-tuned to prevent unnecessary account lockouts, network restrictions, or data loss. Organizations should implement approval-based workflows for high-impact response actions, allowing human analysts to review and confirm automated recommendations before execution. This hybrid approach ensures that automation enhances security operations while maintaining control over critical decision-making processes.

SOAR is transforming cybersecurity operations by enabling organizations to automate security workflows, orchestrate incident response, and integrate threat intelligence for faster and more effective threat mitigation. By leveraging playbooks, automated threat enrichment, and case management capabilities, SOAR solutions reduce the workload on security teams while improving the accuracy and consistency of security responses. As cyber threats continue to evolve, organizations that implement SOAR gain a competitive advantage by enhancing their security posture, reducing response times, and improving overall operational efficiency. By combining automation with human expertise, SOAR platforms empower security teams to stay ahead of modern cyber threats and maintain a resilient security infrastructure.

Managing False Positives in SIEM Alerts

False positives in Security Information and Event Management (SIEM) systems are one of the biggest challenges faced by security teams. A false positive occurs when a SIEM system generates an alert for an event that appears to be suspicious but is actually benign. These unnecessary alerts can overwhelm security analysts, reduce operational efficiency, and increase the risk of real threats being overlooked due to alert fatigue. While SIEM platforms are designed to detect potential security incidents by analyzing logs, correlating events, and applying predefined rules, an excessive number of false positives can reduce their effectiveness. Properly managing and minimizing false positives is essential for improving the accuracy and efficiency of security operations.

One of the primary reasons SIEM systems generate false positives is the use of overly broad or misconfigured correlation rules. Many SIEM deployments rely on predefined detection rules that flag security events based on static thresholds, such as a set number of failed login attempts or access attempts to restricted resources. However, not all of these detected activities indicate a true security threat. For example, a legitimate user may enter their password incorrectly multiple times before successfully logging in, triggering a brute-force alert. To reduce false positives, organizations must fine-tune SIEM correlation rules to align with normal business operations while still detecting genuine security threats.

Customizing and refining detection rules based on historical data and behavioral patterns is an effective way to manage false positives. Instead of applying static rules that treat all failed login attempts equally, security teams can implement dynamic thresholds that take into account factors such as user roles, typical working hours, geographic locations, and device types. If a user commonly logs in from a corporate office and suddenly attempts to authenticate from an unfamiliar location, the SIEM system can factor in the deviation from normal behavior before triggering an alert. By incorporating contextual awareness into correlation rules, organizations can improve the precision of threat detection and reduce unnecessary alerts.

Machine learning and behavioral analytics play a critical role in managing false positives in SIEM alerts. Traditional rule-based detection methods often fail to adapt to evolving attack techniques and user behavior variations. Machine learning models analyze historical security event data to identify normal activity patterns and distinguish between benign and malicious behavior. User and Entity Behavior Analytics (UEBA) enhances SIEM capabilities by establishing baselines for each user and system entity, flagging only significant deviations. If an employee regularly accesses a database at a specific time each day, a minor variation in login time should not trigger an alert. However, if the same user suddenly downloads a large volume of sensitive files outside of their usual working hours, the SIEM system can escalate the event for further investigation.

Fine-tuning alert thresholds is another crucial step in managing false positives. Many SIEM platforms allow security teams to configure alert sensitivity based on risk levels. Setting thresholds too low may generate an excessive number of false positives, while setting them too high could result in missing actual security threats. Organizations should periodically review alert thresholds, adjusting them based on past incidents, business operations, and emerging security risks. Conducting regular audits of SIEM alerts helps identify patterns of false positives and refine detection logic accordingly. Implementing adaptive alerting mechanisms that adjust thresholds dynamically based on system behavior further reduces unnecessary alerts while maintaining security effectiveness.

Integrating SIEM with threat intelligence feeds can help validate alerts and minimize false positives. External threat intelligence sources provide real-time information on known malicious IP addresses, domains, and attack signatures. When a SIEM system detects an event that matches a known indicator of compromise (IOC), it can compare the event against threat intelligence data to determine its legitimacy. If a login attempt originates from an IP address that has been flagged in a threat intelligence database as associated with botnet activity, the SIEM system can prioritize the alert for investigation. Conversely, if an event does not match any known threats, it can be deprioritized to reduce unnecessary noise.

Automating incident response workflows through Security Orchestration, Automation, and Response (SOAR) platforms further assists in managing false positives. When a SIEM alert is triggered, automated workflows can perform additional validation steps before escalating the incident to security analysts. For example, if a SIEM system detects an unusual login attempt, an automated SOAR workflow can verify whether the user recently reset their password or used a new device before flagging the event as a potential threat. By applying automated decision-making processes, SOAR helps reduce analyst workload and ensures that only high-confidence alerts receive immediate attention.

Security teams should also establish clear processes for investigating and categorizing false positives. Documenting common false positive scenarios allows analysts to create suppression rules or refine detection criteria to prevent recurring unnecessary alerts. Implementing a feedback loop where analysts annotate alerts as false positives or legitimate threats helps improve SIEM rule accuracy over time. By analyzing past alerts and refining detection rules based on analyst feedback, organizations can continuously improve SIEM effectiveness and reduce noise in security monitoring.

Reducing false positives requires collaboration between security analysts, IT teams, and business stakeholders. SIEM configurations should reflect real-world business processes to avoid flagging routine activities as suspicious. Security teams should work closely with IT administrators to ensure that log sources, authentication mechanisms, and network configurations are properly aligned with SIEM detection rules. For example, if employees regularly use VPN connections to access corporate systems remotely, the SIEM system should account for this behavior rather than generating alerts for every remote login. Business context must be incorporated into security monitoring to differentiate between legitimate activities and actual security incidents.

Regular testing and validation of SIEM alerts are necessary to maintain optimal performance. Security teams should conduct periodic red team exercises and penetration testing to simulate real-world attacks and assess how well the SIEM system detects genuine threats while avoiding false positives. Simulated attack scenarios help identify gaps in correlation rules and detection logic, allowing organizations to make necessary adjustments. Continuous monitoring and fine-tuning ensure that SIEM remains effective in identifying security incidents while minimizing unnecessary alerts.

Managing false positives in SIEM alerts is an ongoing process that requires a combination of rule refinement, machine learning, threat intelligence integration, automated validation workflows, and collaboration between security teams. By optimizing alert thresholds, leveraging behavioral analytics, and implementing adaptive detection techniques, organizations can significantly reduce false positives while maintaining a strong security posture. A well-tuned SIEM system ensures that security analysts focus on genuine threats, improving response times, operational efficiency, and overall cybersecurity resilience. Properly managing false positives enables organizations to maximize the value of their SIEM investment while reducing alert fatigue and enhancing security monitoring effectiveness.

SIEM Reporting and Dashboards

SIEM reporting and dashboards are essential components of a Security Information and Event Management (SIEM) system, providing security teams with real-time visibility into an organization's security posture. SIEM solutions collect, process, and analyze large volumes of security event data from multiple sources, and the ability to present this data in an understandable and actionable format is critical. Effective reporting and dashboard functionalities enable security analysts, IT administrators, and executives to monitor key security metrics, track incident trends, identify threats, and ensure compliance with regulatory requirements. Well-designed dashboards and reports streamline security operations by offering a centralized view of security events, reducing response times, and improving overall situational awareness.

Dashboards serve as the primary interface for SIEM users, displaying a real-time summary of security events, alerts, and threat intelligence. A well-configured SIEM dashboard consolidates data from firewalls, intrusion detection systems, endpoint security solutions, authentication logs, cloud services, and network traffic monitoring tools. Security teams can customize dashboards to display relevant metrics based on their specific needs, such as the number of active threats, failed login attempts, suspicious file transfers, or ongoing incident investigations. By providing a visual representation of security data, dashboards enable analysts to quickly assess potential risks and take immediate action.

One of the key features of a SIEM dashboard is the ability to display security event trends over time. Historical data analysis helps organizations identify patterns, detect anomalies, and assess the effectiveness of security controls. If an organization experiences a sudden increase in phishing attempts, the SIEM dashboard can highlight this trend, allowing security teams to adjust their email filtering policies and conduct employee awareness training. By tracking the frequency and severity of security incidents, dashboards help organizations measure the impact of security initiatives and adjust their defense strategies accordingly.

SIEM dashboards should include customizable widgets that allow security teams to focus on specific areas of interest. Different teams within an organization may require different views of security data. For example, security analysts may need a dashboard that displays active alerts, open investigations, and correlation rule performance, while compliance officers may require dashboards that track log retention, audit trail completeness, and regulatory compliance metrics. The ability to tailor dashboards ensures that each team has access to the most relevant information without being overwhelmed by unnecessary data.

Threat intelligence integration enhances the effectiveness of SIEM dashboards by providing contextual information about detected security threats. SIEM solutions can incorporate external threat intelligence feeds that identify known malicious IP addresses, domains, and attack signatures. When a security event matches an indicator of compromise (IOC), the SIEM dashboard can highlight the potential threat and provide additional details, such as threat actor profiles, attack methods, and remediation recommendations. By integrating threat intelligence, SIEM dashboards help security teams prioritize alerts based on real-world threat data, reducing false positives and improving response efficiency.

Real-time alerting is another critical aspect of SIEM dashboards, enabling security teams to respond to incidents as they occur. SIEM solutions can be configured to trigger notifications for high-priority security events, such as unauthorized access attempts, data exfiltration, or ransomware activity. Dashboards provide a live feed of critical security events, ensuring that analysts can quickly identify and investigate emerging threats. Color-coded alert severity levels help prioritize incidents, with critical alerts displayed prominently to ensure immediate attention. By providing real-time threat visibility, SIEM dashboards empower security teams to take proactive measures before incidents escalate.

SIEM reporting capabilities complement dashboards by providing in-depth analysis of security trends, incident investigations, and compliance adherence. Reports help organizations document security incidents, track vulnerabilities, and generate executive summaries for management and regulatory authorities. Security teams can use SIEM-generated reports to conduct post-incident reviews, analyze attack vectors, and refine security policies based on past incidents. Reports also play a crucial role in demonstrating compliance with industry regulations such as GDPR, HIPAA, PCI DSS, and NIST.

Automated report generation reduces the manual effort required for security audits and compliance assessments. SIEM solutions allow organizations to schedule reports on a daily, weekly, or monthly basis, ensuring that security teams receive regular insights into security trends and system performance. Compliance reports provide details on log retention, access control enforcement, and security control effectiveness, helping organizations meet regulatory obligations. Audit logs and forensic reports provide detailed event histories that assist in investigating security incidents and ensuring accountability.

Customizable reporting templates allow organizations to tailor SIEM reports based on their specific needs. Executive reports provide high-level summaries of security incidents, highlighting key metrics such as the number of detected threats, response times, and overall security improvements. Security operations reports focus on technical details, including firewall activity, endpoint security alerts, network traffic anomalies, and incident resolution workflows. Compliance reports detail log management practices, incident tracking, and adherence to industry security standards. By offering flexible reporting options, SIEM solutions enable organizations to generate insights that align with their security objectives.

Dashboards and reports also facilitate security benchmarking, allowing organizations to compare their security performance against industry standards and internal key performance indicators (KPIs). By analyzing historical data, SIEM solutions can help organizations identify areas for improvement, measure the effectiveness of security investments, and track progress over time. Security teams can use benchmarking reports to assess the impact of new security controls, evaluate the effectiveness of threat detection mechanisms, and refine incident response processes.

Visualization tools enhance the readability of SIEM dashboards and reports, making complex security data more accessible to both technical and non-technical stakeholders. Graphs, heat maps, and trend lines provide intuitive representations of security metrics, helping decision-makers quickly grasp the significance of security events. Interactive dashboards allow users to drill down into specific data points, enabling more detailed investigations and root cause analysis. By presenting security data in a visually engaging manner, SIEM dashboards and reports improve situational awareness and support informed decision-making.

Managing dashboard performance is essential to ensure that SIEM solutions provide real-time insights without delays. Large-scale organizations generate massive volumes of security logs, and poorly optimized dashboards can suffer from slow query performance and data processing bottlenecks. SIEM administrators must implement indexing strategies, efficient data storage practices, and optimized query execution methods to maintain dashboard responsiveness. Real-time data streaming and caching mechanisms help improve performance by ensuring that dashboards display the latest security information without significant lag.

Continuous refinement of SIEM dashboards and reports is necessary to adapt to evolving security threats and organizational needs. Security teams should regularly review dashboard configurations, update alerting rules, and refine reporting templates to ensure that SIEM solutions remain aligned with business objectives. User feedback is essential in optimizing dashboard layouts and report structures to improve usability and relevance. By continuously enhancing SIEM reporting and visualization capabilities, organizations can maximize the value of their security monitoring efforts and improve overall threat detection efficiency.

SIEM reporting and dashboards play a vital role in cybersecurity operations, providing security teams with the visibility and insights needed to detect, analyze, and respond to threats effectively. By consolidating security event data, integrating threat intelligence, automating report generation, and leveraging data visualization techniques, SIEM solutions enable organizations to maintain a proactive security posture. Customizable dashboards and reports help security teams streamline investigations, optimize security controls, and ensure compliance with industry regulations. Organizations that effectively utilize SIEM reporting and dashboard capabilities can enhance situational awareness, improve incident response times, and strengthen overall cybersecurity resilience.

SIEM Metrics and Key Performance Indicators (KPIs)

Measuring the effectiveness of a Security Information and Event Management (SIEM) system is essential for ensuring that it provides value to an organization's security operations. SIEM solutions collect and analyze vast amounts of security data, but without well-defined metrics and key performance indicators (KPIs), it can be difficult to assess their efficiency, accuracy, and overall impact on cybersecurity. Establishing the right SIEM metrics allows security teams to monitor system performance, evaluate detection capabilities, measure response times, and ensure compliance with security policies. By tracking and optimizing these metrics, organizations can enhance their threat detection, improve incident response, and maximize the return on investment (ROI) in their SIEM deployment.

One of the fundamental SIEM metrics is the total number of security events processed within a given timeframe. SIEM systems ingest logs from firewalls, intrusion detection systems, endpoint security tools, authentication services, and cloud applications. Monitoring the volume of ingested events helps security teams understand the system's workload and assess whether it is capable of handling large-scale data processing. If the number of collected logs exceeds the SIEM system's capacity, it may lead to delayed event correlation, missed alerts, and performance bottlenecks. Optimizing log collection by filtering redundant data and prioritizing critical sources helps maintain efficient SIEM operations.

Event correlation efficiency is another crucial metric that measures how effectively the SIEM system links related security events to identify attack patterns. A well-configured SIEM should correlate logs from multiple sources and generate meaningful alerts when suspicious activities occur. If event correlation is not optimized, security teams may receive fragmented alerts that do not provide sufficient context for identifying threats. By tracking the correlation rate and adjusting detection rules, organizations can improve the accuracy of security event analysis, reducing the likelihood of missing coordinated attack attempts.

False positive and false negative rates are essential KPIs for evaluating SIEM accuracy. False positives occur when the SIEM system generates an alert for a benign event, leading to wasted time and unnecessary investigations. A high false positive rate can overwhelm security analysts and contribute to alert fatigue, reducing their ability to respond effectively to real threats. On the other hand, false negatives occur when the SIEM system fails to detect an actual security incident, allowing threats to go unnoticed. Balancing false positives and false negatives is critical for maintaining a SIEM system that detects real threats while minimizing unnecessary noise. Fine-tuning correlation rules, incorporating user behavior analytics, and integrating threat intelligence feeds help improve the accuracy of threat detection.

Mean time to detect (MTTD) is a key performance indicator that measures how long it takes for a SIEM system to identify a security incident. A low MTTD indicates that threats are detected quickly, allowing security teams to respond before significant damage occurs. A high MTTD suggests inefficiencies in event processing, detection rules, or data correlation. Improving MTTD requires optimizing log ingestion, refining detection logic, and leveraging machine learning to identify anomalies in real time. Organizations should continuously track MTTD to ensure that their SIEM system is operating at peak efficiency.

Mean time to respond (MTTR) is another critical metric that tracks how long it takes for security teams to investigate and remediate a detected threat. A fast response time minimizes the impact of security incidents and reduces the risk of data breaches. MTTR is influenced by factors such as alert prioritization, incident response workflows, and automation capabilities. Security Orchestration, Automation, and Response (SOAR) platforms can help reduce MTTR by automating repetitive response actions, such as isolating compromised devices, revoking access credentials, and blocking malicious network traffic. Monitoring MTTR allows organizations to identify bottlenecks in their incident response process and improve security team efficiency.

The number of critical incidents detected is a KPI that helps organizations measure the severity of security threats identified by the SIEM system. Security teams should categorize incidents based on their impact, such as low, medium, high, and critical. Tracking the frequency of critical incidents over time provides insight into whether an organization is experiencing an increase in targeted attacks, insider threats, or system vulnerabilities. If critical incident rates are rising, it may indicate that security defenses need to be strengthened or that SIEM detection rules need to be adjusted to better identify evolving threats.

Alert triage effectiveness is an important metric for evaluating how efficiently security analysts handle SIEM alerts. SIEM solutions generate a high volume of alerts, but not all alerts require immediate action. Measuring the percentage of alerts that result in confirmed security incidents versus those that are dismissed as false positives provides insight into the accuracy of SIEM detection capabilities. If too many alerts are being dismissed without further investigation, it may indicate gaps in threat detection logic. Conversely, if analysts spend too much time investigating low-priority alerts, it may suggest a need to refine alert prioritization and filtering mechanisms.

Log retention and compliance reporting metrics are crucial for organizations that must adhere to regulatory requirements. Many industries, such as finance, healthcare, and government, have strict regulations that mandate the retention of security logs for a specified period. Tracking log retention metrics ensures that the SIEM system is storing logs in accordance with compliance requirements. Automated compliance reporting helps security teams demonstrate adherence to regulations such as GDPR, HIPAA, PCI DSS, and ISO 27001. By monitoring compliance-related SIEM metrics, organizations can avoid legal penalties and improve audit readiness.

System uptime and performance reliability are technical KPIs that measure the stability and efficiency of a SIEM system. A SIEM platform must operate continuously to provide real-time security monitoring. Downtime or performance issues can create blind spots in security monitoring, increasing the risk of undetected threats. Tracking system uptime, query response times, and processing speed ensures that SIEM remains a reliable component of the security infrastructure. If performance issues arise, optimizing storage, improving indexing strategies, and scaling resources can help maintain smooth SIEM operations.

Threat hunting success rate is a proactive KPI that measures how often security teams successfully identify and mitigate threats before they cause harm. Threat hunting involves actively searching for hidden threats within an organization's network by analyzing SIEM logs and security data. A high threat hunting success rate indicates that the organization is effectively using SIEM for proactive security, while a low success rate may suggest a need for additional training, better visibility, or improved analytics capabilities. By continuously tracking this metric, organizations can refine their threat-hunting strategies and improve their ability to detect advanced cyber threats.

SIEM metrics and KPIs provide organizations with valuable insights into security effectiveness, system performance, and operational efficiency. By tracking metrics such as event correlation efficiency, false positive rates, MTTD, MTTR, and compliance adherence, security teams can optimize their SIEM deployment to enhance threat detection and incident response. Well-defined KPIs ensure that SIEM solutions deliver measurable value, helping organizations strengthen their cybersecurity defenses, reduce risks, and improve overall security posture. Continuous monitoring and refinement of SIEM metrics enable organizations to adapt to evolving threats and maintain a high level of security resilience.

Case Studies: Successful SIEM Deployments

Implementing a Security Information and Event Management (SIEM) system successfully requires careful planning, integration, and optimization to meet an organization's unique security needs. Many organizations across different industries have leveraged SIEM solutions to enhance threat detection, streamline compliance, and improve incident response. Examining real-world case studies of successful SIEM deployments provides valuable insights into best practices, challenges encountered, and the impact of effective SIEM implementation. By analyzing these deployments, organizations can better understand how to maximize the value of their SIEM investment and achieve stronger cybersecurity resilience.

A multinational financial institution faced significant challenges in monitoring its vast IT infrastructure, which included thousands of endpoints, cloud services, and third-party payment processors. The bank struggled with an overwhelming number of security alerts, many of which were false positives, leading to inefficient use of its security operations center (SOC) resources. After deploying a SIEM solution with integrated machine learning-based analytics and behavioral monitoring, the organization was able to reduce false positives by 60 percent. The SIEM system enabled automated correlation of security events across multiple platforms, allowing analysts to identify real threats more quickly. The bank also leveraged threat intelligence feeds to enhance real-time threat detection. Within the first six months of deployment, the institution prevented multiple phishing attacks and unauthorized access attempts that could have led to financial fraud.

A large healthcare provider implemented SIEM to comply with stringent regulations such as HIPAA, which mandates strict access controls and audit logging of patient data. Before SIEM deployment, the organization struggled with manual log analysis and inconsistent security monitoring across its hospital network, clinics, and remote telemedicine services. By integrating SIEM with its electronic health record (EHR) system, firewall logs, and endpoint security tools, the healthcare provider gained real-time visibility into potential security threats. The SIEM solution helped detect insider threats by identifying unusual access patterns to patient records, preventing unauthorized data exfiltration. The automated compliance reporting capabilities of the SIEM system also reduced audit preparation time by 70 percent, enabling the security team to focus more on proactive threat detection rather than administrative tasks.

A government agency responsible for national cybersecurity implemented a SIEM solution to monitor and protect critical infrastructure from cyber threats. Given the highly sensitive nature of its data, the agency required a SIEM platform capable of handling large-scale log ingestion while ensuring real-time threat intelligence integration. The deployment involved connecting SIEM with intrusion detection systems, network traffic analysis tools, and endpoint protection solutions. Within the first year of deployment, the SIEM system successfully detected multiple nation-state cyberattacks, including attempts to infiltrate government databases through spear-phishing campaigns. The automated incident response capabilities of the SIEM platform allowed security analysts to contain threats faster by blocking malicious IP addresses and isolating compromised devices. By leveraging SIEM, the agency strengthened its cybersecurity posture and improved collaboration with international cyber defense partners.

A global e-commerce company deployed a SIEM solution to improve fraud detection and protect customer payment data. The organization experienced frequent account takeover attempts, where cybercriminals used stolen credentials to access customer accounts and make fraudulent transactions. The SIEM system was integrated with the company's identity and access management (IAM) platform, payment processing systems, and web application firewall. By using SIEM to analyze login behaviors and transaction patterns, the company detected anomalies such as sudden login attempts from high-risk geographic regions followed by large purchases. The SIEM system triggered automated response actions, including requiring multi-factor authentication (MFA) for suspicious logins and blocking high-risk transactions before they could be processed. As a result, the company reduced fraud-related financial losses by 40 percent and significantly improved customer trust in its security measures.

A major manufacturing company with operations across multiple continents faced security challenges due to the complexity of its supply chain and industrial control systems (ICS). The company deployed a SIEM system to monitor its IT and operational technology (OT) environments, ensuring protection against cyber threats targeting industrial processes. The SIEM platform was configured to collect logs from ICS devices, supervisory control and data acquisition (SCADA) systems, and traditional IT security tools. Within months of deployment, the SIEM system detected a targeted ransomware attack attempting to encrypt production control systems. The automated incident response workflow isolated the affected segment of the network, preventing the attack from spreading and avoiding costly production downtime. By leveraging SIEM for OT security monitoring, the company minimized operational disruptions and strengthened the resilience of its manufacturing processes against cyber threats.

A large retail chain successfully deployed a SIEM system to combat point-of-sale (POS) malware and enhance data security across its stores. Prior to SIEM implementation, the company struggled with detecting unauthorized access to its POS terminals and monitoring payment card data security. The SIEM system was integrated with endpoint detection and response (EDR) solutions, network traffic logs, and employee access management systems. The retailer used SIEM analytics to identify suspicious behaviors, such as unauthorized remote access to POS terminals or attempts to install unknown software on cash register systems. The SIEM system provided security teams with real-time alerts whenever anomalies were detected, enabling them to respond before customer payment data was compromised. Over the course of a year, the SIEM deployment helped prevent multiple attempted breaches, strengthening the retailer's compliance with the Payment Card Industry Data Security Standard (PCI DSS) and reducing the risk of costly data breaches.

A technology firm specializing in software-as-a-service (SaaS) solutions implemented a SIEM system to protect its cloud-based applications from cyber threats. The company needed a scalable SIEM solution capable of monitoring multi-cloud environments, including Amazon Web Services (AWS), Microsoft Azure, and Google Cloud Platform (GCP). By integrating SIEM with cloud-native security tools, the company gained visibility into cloud access logs, API activity, and suspicious data movements. The SIEM system helped detect misconfigured cloud storage permissions that could have exposed customer data. Automated remediation workflows were implemented to enforce security policies, preventing future misconfigurations. Additionally, the SIEM platform improved DevSecOps processes by integrating with development pipelines, allowing security teams to detect vulnerabilities in application code before deployment. The implementation of SIEM strengthened the company's cloud security posture and reduced the risk of data exposure in its SaaS offerings.

A university deployed a SIEM solution to enhance cybersecurity awareness and protect student and faculty data. The institution had faced repeated attempts to compromise its network through phishing campaigns targeting faculty email accounts. The SIEM system was configured to analyze email security logs, detect suspicious login patterns, and identify potential credential theft attempts. The system flagged phishing-related incidents early, allowing security teams to take action before attackers could gain access to sensitive research data. Additionally, SIEM reports provided insights into cyber threats targeting the education sector, helping IT administrators strengthen security awareness programs. By integrating SIEM with security training initiatives, the university reduced phishing-related security incidents by 50 percent and improved overall cybersecurity awareness among faculty and students.

These case studies demonstrate how successful SIEM deployments can transform security operations across different industries. By integrating SIEM with existing security tools, automating incident response, leveraging threat intelligence, and fine-tuning detection capabilities, organizations have enhanced their ability to detect and mitigate threats efficiently. Effective SIEM implementations provide real-time security visibility, reduce incident response times, improve compliance adherence, and protect critical assets from cyber threats. Organizations looking to deploy SIEM can learn from these success stories and tailor their implementation strategies to maximize the effectiveness of their security monitoring efforts.

Troubleshooting Common SIEM Issues

Implementing and maintaining a Security Information and Event Management (SIEM) system presents various challenges that can affect its efficiency, accuracy, and performance. While SIEM solutions provide critical capabilities for threat detection, compliance monitoring, and incident response, organizations often encounter technical and operational issues that require troubleshooting. Understanding common SIEM problems and their solutions helps security teams optimize system performance, reduce false positives, improve threat detection, and ensure the reliability of security monitoring. Addressing these challenges proactively minimizes disruptions in security operations and enhances the effectiveness of a SIEM deployment.

One of the most frequent issues in SIEM deployments is poor log collection and ingestion. SIEM systems rely on logs from multiple sources, including firewalls, intrusion detection systems, endpoint security tools, and cloud services. If logs are missing, incomplete, or improperly formatted, SIEM may fail to detect security incidents accurately. To troubleshoot log collection problems, security teams should verify that all log sources are properly configured to send data to the SIEM platform. Checking for connectivity issues, ensuring that log forwarding mechanisms such as syslog and API integrations are functioning correctly, and confirming that timestamps are synchronized across all devices helps prevent data gaps. Additionally, reviewing SIEM ingestion settings and increasing log buffer capacity can prevent dropped events due to high log volume.

Another common problem is excessive false positives, which can overwhelm security analysts and reduce operational efficiency. False positives occur when the SIEM system generates alerts for benign activities that do not indicate actual security threats. This often happens when correlation rules are too broad, threshold settings are too low, or behavioral baselines are not properly defined. To reduce false positives, security teams should fine-tune correlation rules by incorporating contextual factors such as user behavior, device type, and network location. Implementing machine learning-based anomaly detection and integrating external threat intelligence feeds can help refine detection accuracy by filtering out non-threatening activities.

Regularly reviewing alert data, adjusting rule parameters, and using risk-based alert scoring ensure that security analysts focus on high-priority threats instead of wasting time on non-critical alerts.

Performance issues, such as slow query execution and delayed alerting, can significantly impact the effectiveness of a SIEM system. When SIEM platforms process large volumes of security event data, inefficient storage, indexing, and search mechanisms may cause latency. To troubleshoot slow performance, security teams should optimize database indexing, configure time-based data partitioning, and ensure that log storage solutions are scalable. Upgrading hardware resources, implementing distributed processing for log analysis, and using high-speed storage such as solid-state drives (SSDs) improve SIEM responsiveness. Additionally, adjusting retention policies to move older logs to archival storage while keeping recent logs in high-performance storage enhances query efficiency.

Failure to correlate security events correctly is another challenge that affects SIEM detection capabilities. Correlation rules are designed to link related security events and identify attack patterns, but misconfigured rules or incomplete data can result in missed detections. Security teams should regularly review correlation logic, ensuring that event relationships are properly defined and that logs from all necessary sources are available for correlation. Testing correlation rules using simulated attack scenarios helps validate detection accuracy and fine-tune rule effectiveness. Additionally, using advanced correlation techniques such as sequence-based event analysis and risk-based prioritization improves SIEM's ability to detect sophisticated cyber threats.

Integration issues with third-party security tools can also create challenges in SIEM deployments. Many organizations integrate SIEM with endpoint detection and response (EDR) solutions, threat intelligence platforms, security orchestration, automation, and response (SOAR) systems, and cloud security services. If these integrations fail, security teams may experience gaps in security monitoring and incident response. To troubleshoot integration failures, administrators should verify API configurations, ensure that authentication tokens and credentials are correctly set up, and check for software compatibility issues. Monitoring integration logs and reviewing SIEM connectors for errors helps identify misconfigurations that may be causing data transfer failures. Regularly updating integration modules and testing interoperability with third-party security tools prevents disruptions in SIEM functionality.

Another common SIEM issue is data overload, which occurs when the system ingests excessive log data that overwhelms storage capacity and slows down processing. Many organizations configure their SIEM to collect logs from all available sources, but not all logs are equally valuable for threat detection. Security teams should implement log filtering strategies to prioritize high-value security events while excluding low-risk logs that do not provide meaningful security insights. Defining log collection policies based on compliance requirements, threat detection needs, and retention guidelines helps balance data volume and SIEM performance. Implementing data deduplication and compression further reduces storage consumption without sacrificing critical security data.

Failure to detect insider threats is another challenge that organizations face when using SIEM. Traditional SIEM implementations primarily focus on detecting external attacks, but insider threats require behavioral analytics and user activity monitoring. To improve insider threat detection, security teams should integrate user and entity behavior analytics (UEBA) with SIEM to establish behavioral baselines for employees and privileged users. Monitoring deviations from normal behavior, such as unauthorized access attempts, unusual working hours, and excessive data transfers, helps detect insider threats early. Implementing real-time alerts for privilege escalations, file access anomalies, and unauthorized data movements enhances SIEM's capability to mitigate insider risks.

Compliance reporting errors are another issue that organizations may encounter when using SIEM to meet regulatory requirements. Many industry regulations, such as GDPR, HIPAA, and PCI DSS, require organizations to generate audit logs, maintain data retention policies, and produce compliance reports. If SIEM reports fail to capture required security events or if log retention policies do not meet regulatory standards, organizations may face compliance violations. Security teams should regularly review reporting configurations, validate data completeness, and ensure that compliance reports align with regulatory mandates. Automating report generation and scheduling periodic compliance audits within the SIEM system help maintain compliance readiness.

SIEM misconfigurations are a common cause of operational inefficiencies and detection failures. Many organizations deploy SIEM with default settings without customizing configurations to their specific security needs. Reviewing and optimizing SIEM settings, including log source configurations, event correlation rules, alerting policies, and retention schedules, ensures that the system operates efficiently. Conducting regular SIEM health checks, testing detection rules, and fine-tuning alert workflows helps organizations maintain an effective security monitoring system.

Maintaining SIEM scalability as an organization grows is another challenge that security teams must address. As businesses expand their IT infrastructure, SIEM log ingestion and analysis workloads increase. Organizations must ensure that their SIEM solution is designed to scale dynamically by leveraging cloud-based storage, distributed processing, and modular architecture. Monitoring system resource utilization, implementing load balancing, and expanding storage capacity as needed prevents performance bottlenecks.

Proactive troubleshooting and continuous optimization are essential for ensuring that SIEM systems function efficiently and provide accurate security monitoring. Security teams should conduct periodic assessments, refine detection logic, optimize performance settings, and integrate automation to enhance SIEM effectiveness. By addressing common issues such as log collection failures, false positives, performance slowdowns, event correlation errors, and compliance challenges, organizations can maximize the value of their SIEM investment and improve overall cybersecurity resilience.

Future Trends in SIEM Technology

As cyber threats continue to evolve, Security Information and Event Management (SIEM) technology is undergoing significant advancements to keep pace with the changing security landscape. Organizations are facing increasingly complex threats, ranging from sophisticated ransomware attacks to advanced persistent threats

(APTs), requiring SIEM solutions to become more adaptive, intelligent, and scalable. Emerging trends in SIEM technology focus on improving real-time threat detection, automating incident response, enhancing integration with cloud environments, leveraging artificial intelligence, and optimizing security analytics. These innovations are transforming how security teams use SIEM to protect digital assets, improve operational efficiency, and strengthen overall cybersecurity posture.

Artificial intelligence (AI) and machine learning (ML) are playing an increasingly critical role in SIEM evolution. Traditional SIEM systems rely on static correlation rules and predefined signatures to detect threats, but these methods often struggle to identify emerging attack techniques. AI-driven SIEM solutions leverage ML algorithms to analyze vast amounts of security data, detect anomalies, and predict potential threats based on behavioral patterns. By continuously learning from historical security events, machine learning models improve threat detection accuracy while reducing false positives. User and Entity Behavior Analytics (UEBA) is one of the key applications of AI in SIEM, enabling systems to establish behavioral baselines and detect deviations that may indicate insider threats, compromised credentials, or unauthorized access attempts. The integration of AI-driven threat detection reduces the reliance on manual rule tuning and enhances security teams' ability to respond to unknown threats.

Cloud-native SIEM solutions are becoming a dominant trend as organizations increasingly migrate workloads to cloud environments. Traditional SIEM platforms were designed for on-premises infrastructure, often requiring complex configurations to collect logs from cloud services. Cloud-native SIEM solutions, built specifically for cloud environments, offer seamless integration with platforms such as Amazon Web Services (AWS), Microsoft Azure, and Google Cloud Platform (GCP). These solutions leverage cloud scalability, real-time analytics, and API-based log collection to provide continuous security monitoring. Cloud SIEM eliminates infrastructure maintenance overhead, allowing organizations to focus on security operations rather than managing hardware and storage limitations. The adoption of serverless architectures and distributed computing further enhances the scalability and cost-effectiveness of cloud SIEM, making it a preferred choice for organizations with dynamic IT environments.

Automation and orchestration are becoming essential components of next-generation SIEM technology. Security teams face alert fatigue due to the high volume of security events generated daily, making it challenging to prioritize and respond to threats effectively. Security Orchestration, Automation, and Response (SOAR) platforms are increasingly being integrated with SIEM solutions to streamline incident response workflows. By automating repetitive security tasks, such as log analysis, alert triage, and threat containment, SOAR-enabled SIEM systems reduce response times and improve efficiency. Automated playbooks enable SIEM to take predefined actions when specific threats are detected, such as blocking malicious IP addresses, disabling compromised accounts, or isolating infected endpoints. This level of automation enhances security team productivity while ensuring a faster and more coordinated response to security incidents.

Threat intelligence integration is another significant advancement in SIEM technology. Modern SIEM platforms are incorporating real-time threat intelligence feeds to improve detection capabilities and provide contextual awareness of security threats. Threat intelligence feeds aggregate data from multiple sources, including government agencies, cybersecurity research groups, and industry-specific Information Sharing and Analysis Centers (ISACs). By correlating internal security events with external threat intelligence, SIEM systems can identify emerging threats, detect indicators of compromise (IOCs), and prioritize high-risk alerts. The future of SIEM will likely involve deeper integration with global threat intelligence platforms, leveraging AI-driven threat intelligence analytics to provide predictive insights into potential cyberattacks before they materialize.

Zero Trust architecture is reshaping how SIEM systems approach security monitoring and threat detection. The traditional perimeter-based security model is no longer sufficient as organizations adopt hybrid and multi-cloud environments, enabling remote workforces and expanding attack surfaces. SIEM technology is evolving to align with Zero Trust principles, which emphasize continuous verification, least-privilege access, and micro-segmentation. Future SIEM solutions will incorporate identity-centric security monitoring, analyzing user behaviors, access requests, and privilege escalations in real time. By integrating with identity and access management (IAM) solutions, next-generation SIEM platforms will provide more granular visibility into user activities and detect policy violations that could indicate insider threats or account takeovers.

The convergence of SIEM with extended detection and response (XDR) solutions is another emerging trend. XDR expands the capabilities of SIEM by integrating endpoint, network, and cloud security telemetry into a unified platform. Unlike traditional SIEM, which relies primarily on log aggregation and event correlation, XDR provides advanced threat analytics across multiple attack vectors. By combining SIEM with XDR capabilities, organizations gain a more holistic view of their security environment, enabling faster threat detection and automated response across endpoints, workloads, and cloud applications. This trend is particularly valuable for organizations looking to consolidate security operations while improving detection accuracy.

Security analytics and big data processing are also transforming how SIEM systems handle large-scale security telemetry. Organizations generate massive amounts of security data daily, making it challenging to process logs efficiently while maintaining real-time monitoring capabilities. Next-generation SIEM platforms leverage big data analytics frameworks, such as Apache Hadoop and Apache Spark, to process security logs at scale. The adoption of cloud-based data lakes allows SIEM systems to store and analyze vast amounts of historical security data, enabling long-term threat hunting and forensic investigations. Future SIEM solutions will continue to refine security analytics capabilities, using AI-driven predictive modeling to detect threats before they occur.

Compliance automation is becoming an integral feature of SIEM technology, helping organizations meet regulatory requirements without excessive manual effort. Regulations such as GDPR, HIPAA, PCI DSS, and CMMC require organizations to maintain audit logs, conduct security assessments, and generate compliance reports. SIEM platforms are evolving to provide built-in compliance automation, streamlining log retention, policy enforcement, and audit reporting. By integrating compliance frameworks into SIEM workflows, organizations can ensure continuous adherence to security standards while reducing the complexity of regulatory audits. Future SIEM platforms will likely incorporate AI-driven compliance analytics to detect policy violations in real time and suggest remediation actions.

Decentralized and blockchain-based security monitoring is an emerging concept that could influence the future of SIEM technology. Blockchain offers immutable logging capabilities, ensuring that security events cannot be altered or deleted by attackers. Some security vendors are exploring the use of blockchain for decentralized SIEM log storage, enhancing data integrity and auditability. While still in its early stages, blockchain-driven SIEM solutions may provide a new layer of trust and transparency in security event management, particularly in highly regulated industries where data integrity is paramount.

The future of SIEM technology is shaped by advancements in AI, automation, cloud-native security, Zero Trust adoption, and integrated threat intelligence. As cyber threats continue to evolve, SIEM platforms will become more adaptive, predictive, and automated, enabling organizations to respond to security incidents with greater speed and accuracy. By leveraging emerging technologies and refining security analytics capabilities, SIEM solutions will play a crucial role in protecting organizations from sophisticated cyberattacks while improving security operations efficiency. Organizations that embrace these advancements will be better equipped to detect, analyze, and mitigate security threats in an increasingly complex digital landscape.

The Role of Artificial Intelligence in SIEM

Artificial Intelligence (AI) is revolutionizing Security Information and Event Management (SIEM) by enhancing threat detection, automating security workflows, and improving overall cybersecurity operations. Traditional SIEM systems rely on predefined rules and correlation logic to detect threats, but these methods have limitations when dealing with modern, sophisticated cyberattacks. AI-powered SIEM solutions leverage machine learning (ML), natural language processing (NLP), and behavioral analytics to analyze massive volumes of security data, identify patterns, and predict threats in real time. By incorporating AI, SIEM platforms can become more adaptive, reducing false positives, detecting unknown threats, and accelerating incident response.

One of the most significant applications of AI in SIEM is anomaly detection. Traditional rule-based SIEM systems generate alerts based on predefined thresholds, such as a set number of failed login attempts or unusual data transfers. However, attackers often find ways to evade these static rules by using techniques that mimic normal activity. AI-driven anomaly detection goes beyond simple threshold-based monitoring by continuously analyzing user behavior, network traffic, and system activity to establish baselines of normal behavior. When deviations occur, AI algorithms can detect subtle anomalies that might indicate a potential security breach. For example, if a user who typically logs in from one geographic location suddenly accesses the network from an unusual country, AI can flag the activity as suspicious and prioritize it for investigation.

User and Entity Behavior Analytics (UEBA) is another critical AI-driven enhancement to SIEM. By applying machine learning to user and device activity logs, UEBA helps identify behavioral deviations that could indicate compromised credentials, insider threats, or advanced persistent threats (APTs). AI-powered SIEM solutions analyze historical behavioral patterns to detect anomalies such as excessive login attempts, abnormal file access, or unauthorized privilege escalation. If an employee who typically accesses only internal databases suddenly begins downloading large amounts of sensitive data to an external drive, UEBA can generate an alert. Unlike traditional SIEM systems that rely on fixed rules, AI-powered SIEM continuously refines its understanding of normal behavior, improving accuracy over time.

AI-driven SIEM solutions also improve threat intelligence integration. Cyber threats evolve rapidly, and new attack techniques emerge daily. SIEM systems must process vast amounts of threat intelligence data from multiple sources, including open-source feeds, commercial threat intelligence providers, and government agencies. AI automates the ingestion, analysis, and correlation of threat intelligence, allowing SIEM platforms to prioritize the most relevant threats. Machine learning algorithms can cross-reference security logs with known indicators of compromise (IOCs), identifying potential threats in real time. If a SIEM system detects an outbound connection to an IP address associated with a known malware command-and-control server, AI can automatically trigger a high-priority alert and suggest remediation steps.

Reducing false positives is one of the most significant benefits of AI in SIEM. Traditional SIEM platforms often generate an overwhelming number of alerts, many of which turn out to be benign. Security analysts can become desensitized to alerts, leading to alert fatigue and slower response times. AI-powered SIEM systems use intelligent filtering mechanisms to differentiate between real threats and non-malicious activity. By analyzing past incident data, AI can learn which alerts are typically dismissed as false positives and refine detection rules accordingly. This adaptive learning process allows SIEM to provide more accurate alerts, reducing the burden on security teams and improving overall efficiency.

AI enhances automated incident response capabilities in SIEM by enabling faster and more precise threat mitigation. Security Orchestration, Automation, and Response (SOAR) platforms integrated with AI-powered SIEM solutions can automatically execute response actions based on detected threats. When AI identifies a high-risk security event, it can trigger automated workflows that isolate compromised devices, block malicious IP addresses, and revoke access privileges for affected accounts. AI-driven playbooks can also guide security analysts by providing step-by-step remediation recommendations, ensuring a consistent and effective response to security incidents. By accelerating threat containment, AI-powered SIEM reduces the dwell time of attackers and minimizes potential damage.

Predictive analytics is another key advantage of AI in SIEM. Traditional SIEM solutions operate reactively, identifying threats only after suspicious activity has been detected. AI introduces predictive capabilities by analyzing historical security data to anticipate potential attack patterns before they occur. By detecting early warning signs, such as gradual increases in failed login attempts, subtle privilege escalations, or repeated probing of network defenses, AI can alert security teams to potential attacks before they fully materialize. This proactive approach enables organizations to strengthen defenses, apply targeted security controls, and prevent breaches before they happen.

AI-powered threat hunting capabilities further enhance SIEM's effectiveness by enabling security teams to uncover hidden threats that traditional detection methods might miss. Threat hunting involves proactively searching for indicators of compromise (IOCs) and tactics used by cyber adversaries. AI-driven SIEM solutions assist in threat hunting by analyzing vast datasets, identifying unusual correlations, and suggesting areas for deeper investigation. AI can process unstructured security data, such as logs from endpoints, cloud services, and network traffic, and surface potential attack indicators that might otherwise go unnoticed. By empowering analysts with intelligent search and correlation capabilities, AI enhances an organization's ability to detect and respond to sophisticated threats.

Natural language processing (NLP) is also improving SIEM operations by enabling security analysts to interact with SIEM systems using human-like queries. Instead of writing complex search queries to investigate security incidents, analysts can use NLP-powered interfaces to ask questions such as "Show me all failed login attempts from unauthorized locations in the last 24 hours." AI interprets these requests, retrieves relevant security data, and presents it in an understandable format. This innovation makes SIEM tools more accessible to security teams with varying levels of expertise, reducing the learning curve and improving usability.

The integration of AI into SIEM is also driving advancements in compliance automation. Many industries require organizations to meet strict regulatory requirements for security monitoring, log retention, and incident reporting. AI-powered SIEM solutions can automatically map security events to compliance frameworks such as GDPR, HIPAA, PCI DSS, and NIST. By analyzing logs and security controls, AI can generate compliance reports, identify gaps in regulatory adherence, and suggest corrective actions. Automating compliance monitoring reduces the administrative burden on security teams and ensures that organizations remain audit-ready at all times.

As cyber threats continue to evolve, AI will play an increasingly vital role in the future of SIEM. AI-driven SIEM solutions provide more accurate threat detection, reduce alert fatigue, automate response actions, and enhance predictive security analytics. By leveraging machine learning, behavioral analysis, NLP, and predictive modeling, AI-powered SIEM platforms enable organizations to stay ahead of emerging threats and improve overall cybersecurity resilience. The integration of AI in SIEM represents a significant shift toward smarter, more adaptive security monitoring, ensuring that organizations can effectively defend against both known and unknown cyber threats in an ever-changing digital landscape.

Continuous Monitoring and SIEM Evolution

Continuous monitoring has become a fundamental aspect of modern cybersecurity, enabling organizations to detect, analyze, and respond to security threats in real time. Security Information and Event Management (SIEM) solutions have evolved significantly to support continuous monitoring by integrating advanced analytics, automated response mechanisms, and real-time data correlation. Traditional SIEM systems were primarily designed for log collection, compliance reporting, and post-incident investigation. However, as cyber threats have become more sophisticated, SIEM has transformed into a proactive security platform capable of continuously monitoring IT environments, identifying anomalies, and mitigating risks before they escalate into full-scale security incidents. The evolution of SIEM has been driven by the need for faster threat detection, enhanced scalability, and greater integration with modern IT infrastructures, including cloud environments, hybrid networks, and endpoint security solutions.

One of the key aspects of continuous monitoring in SIEM is the ability to collect and analyze security event data in real time. Organizations generate vast amounts of log data from firewalls, intrusion detection systems, authentication servers, endpoint protection platforms, and cloud applications. Traditional batch-processing methods are no longer sufficient for detecting cyber threats that can unfold within seconds. Modern SIEM solutions leverage streaming analytics and real-time log processing to ensure that security teams receive alerts immediately when suspicious activity is detected. This shift from periodic log analysis to continuous data ingestion allows SIEM systems to provide timely insights, reducing the window of opportunity for attackers.

The integration of machine learning and behavioral analytics has further enhanced continuous monitoring capabilities in SIEM. Traditional rule-based detection mechanisms often struggle to keep up with evolving attack techniques, as static correlation rules cannot adapt to new threats. Machine learning algorithms analyze historical security data, establish behavioral baselines, and detect deviations that may indicate malicious activity. By continuously learning from new security events, machine learning-driven SIEM solutions improve threat detection accuracy while minimizing false positives. Behavioral analytics enables SIEM to monitor user activities, network traffic patterns, and application behavior, identifying anomalies that may signal insider threats, credential-based attacks, or lateral movement within a compromised network.

Cloud security monitoring has become a critical component of SIEM evolution. As organizations migrate workloads to cloud platforms such as Amazon Web Services (AWS), Microsoft Azure, and Google Cloud Platform (GCP), SIEM solutions must adapt to monitor cloud-based assets effectively. Traditional SIEM systems were designed for on-premises environments, making it challenging to collect and analyze logs from cloud-native services. Modern SIEM platforms offer seamless integration with cloud security tools, API-driven log collection, and real-time visibility into cloud activity. Continuous cloud monitoring ensures that security teams can detect misconfigurations, unauthorized access attempts, and data exfiltration in cloud environments. As multi-cloud and hybrid infrastructures become more common, SIEM solutions are evolving to provide unified security monitoring across diverse IT ecosystems.

The adoption of Security Orchestration, Automation, and Response (SOAR) has further advanced SIEM's role in continuous monitoring. SIEM platforms generate a high volume of security alerts, many of which require immediate investigation and remediation. SOAR integration enables SIEM to automate incident response workflows, reducing the burden on security analysts and improving response times. When a security event is detected, SIEM can trigger automated actions such as isolating compromised endpoints, blocking malicious IP addresses, or enforcing access control policies. By combining continuous monitoring with automated response capabilities, SIEM enhances an organization's ability to contain threats before they cause significant damage.

Threat intelligence feeds play an essential role in the evolution of SIEM by providing real-time insights into emerging cyber threats. Modern SIEM solutions integrate with external threat intelligence platforms to correlate security events with known indicators of compromise (IOCs). By continuously updating threat databases with the latest attack signatures, malicious IP addresses, and advanced persistent threat (APT) tactics, SIEM systems improve their ability to detect sophisticated attacks. Threat intelligence-driven SIEM platforms prioritize alerts based on risk levels, helping security teams focus on high-impact threats while reducing noise from low-priority events. Continuous threat intelligence enrichment ensures that SIEM systems remain effective in identifying evolving cyber threats.

Compliance monitoring has also benefited from the evolution of SIEM technology. Many industries, including healthcare, finance, and government, are subject to strict regulatory requirements that mandate continuous security monitoring and audit logging. SIEM solutions help organizations maintain compliance with regulations such as GDPR, HIPAA, PCI DSS, and ISO 27001 by automating log retention, generating compliance reports, and enforcing security policies. Continuous monitoring ensures that organizations can detect policy violations, unauthorized access attempts, and configuration changes that may impact regulatory compliance. Automated compliance reporting reduces the administrative overhead of security audits, allowing organizations to focus on proactive threat management.

Endpoint security monitoring has become a major focus in SIEM evolution, as cybercriminals increasingly target individual devices as entry points into corporate networks. Traditional SIEM implementations primarily focused on network-based threat detection, but modern SIEM solutions incorporate endpoint telemetry to provide a more comprehensive view of security incidents. By integrating with Endpoint Detection and Response (EDR) tools, SIEM platforms collect detailed endpoint activity data, including process executions, file modifications, and registry changes. Continuous monitoring of endpoint behavior enables security teams to detect malware infections, ransomware attacks, and privilege escalation attempts in real time. The convergence of SIEM and EDR enhances security visibility, enabling rapid threat containment at the device level.

The scalability of SIEM solutions has improved significantly with the adoption of cloud-native architectures. Organizations generate exponentially increasing volumes of security data, making it essential for SIEM platforms to scale dynamically. Traditional SIEM deployments often struggled with performance limitations due to hardware constraints and storage capacity issues. Cloud-based SIEM solutions offer elastic scalability, allowing organizations to handle large-scale log ingestion, real-time analytics, and long-term data retention without infrastructure bottlenecks. The shift toward cloud-native SIEM ensures that security teams can continuously monitor expanding IT environments without compromising performance.

Predictive security analytics is shaping the future of SIEM by enabling organizations to anticipate threats before they occur. Instead of solely reacting to detected incidents, predictive analytics uses historical security data to identify trends and potential attack vectors. By applying AI-driven forecasting models, SIEM platforms can predict potential vulnerabilities, detect early-stage attack indicators, and recommend preemptive security measures. Continuous monitoring, combined with predictive analytics, transforms SIEM from a reactive tool into a proactive security intelligence platform.

As cyber threats continue to evolve, SIEM technology is expected to advance further, incorporating deeper automation, AI-driven threat detection, and enhanced integration with security ecosystems. The focus on continuous monitoring ensures that SIEM remains a central component of modern cybersecurity strategies, providing organizations with real-time visibility, automated response capabilities, and predictive analytics to stay ahead of emerging threats. By continuously refining detection algorithms, integrating advanced security telemetry, and leveraging threat intelligence, SIEM solutions will continue to evolve as a cornerstone of enterprise security, helping organizations detect, analyze, and respond to cyber threats with greater efficiency and precision.

SIEM in Small and Medium Enterprises (SMEs)

Security Information and Event Management (SIEM) solutions have traditionally been associated with large enterprises that require complex security monitoring and compliance management. However, small and medium enterprises (SMEs) are increasingly becoming targets for cyberattacks, making SIEM a valuable tool for organizations of all sizes. SMEs often face significant security challenges due to limited resources, smaller IT teams, and a lack of dedicated security personnel. Despite these challenges, implementing SIEM can provide SMEs with essential capabilities for threat detection, log management, and regulatory compliance. As SIEM technology evolves, cost-effective and scalable solutions tailored for SMEs are becoming more accessible, enabling smaller organizations to enhance their cybersecurity posture without requiring extensive budgets or technical expertise.

One of the primary security challenges for SMEs is the growing sophistication of cyber threats. Attackers often perceive SMEs as easy targets because they typically lack the advanced security infrastructure of larger enterprises. Ransomware attacks, phishing campaigns, and credential theft have become major concerns for SMEs, with many organizations suffering financial and reputational damage from security breaches. A SIEM system can help SMEs detect and respond to these threats by continuously monitoring network activity, identifying anomalies, and correlating security events from multiple sources. By implementing SIEM, SMEs gain real-time visibility into their IT environments, allowing them to detect suspicious activity before it leads to a security incident.

Cost has historically been a barrier for SMEs considering SIEM adoption. Traditional SIEM solutions required expensive hardware, dedicated security personnel, and ongoing maintenance, making them impractical for smaller organizations. However, modern cloud-based SIEM solutions have significantly reduced the cost and complexity of implementation. Cloud SIEM platforms eliminate the need for on-premises infrastructure, offering a subscription-based model that allows SMEs to scale security operations based on their needs. With cloud-native SIEM, SMEs can access enterprise-grade security monitoring without the high upfront costs associated with traditional deployments. This shift towards cloud SIEM has made advanced security capabilities more accessible to organizations with limited IT budgets.

Ease of deployment and management is another important factor for SMEs adopting SIEM. Unlike large enterprises that have dedicated security teams, SMEs often rely on general IT staff who may not have specialized cybersecurity expertise. Traditional SIEM implementations required extensive configuration, fine-tuning of correlation rules, and continuous monitoring, which posed a challenge for smaller organizations with limited technical resources. Today, SIEM vendors are offering simplified deployment options with automated log collection, pre-configured security rules, and user-friendly dashboards that make it easier for SMEs to manage security monitoring. Many cloud SIEM solutions also include built-in threat intelligence and machine learning-driven analytics, reducing the need for manual rule configuration and enabling SMEs to detect threats more effectively.

Regulatory compliance is another reason why SMEs are adopting SIEM solutions. Many industries have strict security and data protection requirements, including GDPR, HIPAA, PCI DSS, and ISO 27001. SMEs that process sensitive customer data, financial transactions, or healthcare records must comply with these regulations to avoid legal and financial penalties. SIEM helps SMEs meet compliance requirements by automating log collection, generating audit reports, and tracking access to sensitive data. Compliance automation reduces the burden on SMEs, allowing them to focus on business operations while ensuring that security policies are enforced. Cloud SIEM solutions often include pre-built compliance reporting templates, making it easier for SMEs to generate required documentation for regulatory audits.

Threat detection and incident response are critical functions of SIEM that can help SMEs mitigate cyber risks. Small and medium businesses may not have the resources to hire a dedicated Security Operations Center (SOC), making automated threat detection and response essential. SIEM solutions with integrated Security Orchestration, Automation, and Response (SOAR) capabilities enable SMEs to automate incident response workflows. When SIEM detects a security event, such as an unauthorized login attempt or a malware infection, it can trigger automated actions, such as blocking IP addresses, disabling compromised accounts, or alerting IT personnel. By automating response actions, SIEM allows SMEs to reduce the impact of security incidents and improve response times, even with limited security staff.

Scalability is another advantage of modern SIEM solutions for SMEs. As businesses grow, their IT infrastructure becomes more complex, with additional endpoints, cloud services, and third-party integrations. A scalable SIEM solution allows SMEs to expand security monitoring as their needs evolve. Cloud SIEM platforms offer flexible pricing models that allow organizations to start with a basic deployment and add additional features as their security requirements increase. This flexibility ensures that SMEs can implement SIEM at an affordable cost while retaining the ability to scale up as their cybersecurity needs change.

Integration with existing security tools is a key consideration for SMEs implementing SIEM. Many smaller organizations already use endpoint protection software, firewalls, and cloud security tools but may lack a centralized platform to correlate and analyze security events. SIEM acts as a unifying layer that consolidates security data from different sources, providing a holistic view of potential threats. By integrating with existing security solutions, SIEM enhances threat detection accuracy and enables SMEs to make informed security decisions. Modern SIEM platforms support API-based integrations, allowing seamless connectivity with third-party security tools, cloud services, and identity and access management (IAM) solutions.

User-friendly reporting and visualization are important features that make SIEM accessible to SMEs. Security teams in smaller organizations need clear, actionable insights rather than complex data that requires extensive analysis. Many SIEM platforms now offer intuitive dashboards that present security events, incident trends, and compliance status in an easy-to-understand format. SMEs can customize dashboards to focus on critical security metrics, such as the number of blocked threats, login anomalies, and network traffic anomalies. Automated reporting capabilities allow SMEs to generate executive summaries that provide high-level security insights without requiring deep technical knowledge.

Despite the benefits of SIEM, SMEs may face challenges in optimizing their deployment. One of the most common issues is dealing with false positives, which can overwhelm IT teams with unnecessary alerts. To address this challenge, SMEs should fine-tune SIEM rules based on their specific security environment, filter out irrelevant logs, and leverage machine learning-driven analytics to prioritize high-risk threats. Another challenge is ensuring that SIEM is properly configured to detect advanced threats, such as phishing and insider attacks. Regularly reviewing correlation rules, updating threat intelligence feeds, and conducting simulated attack scenarios can help SMEs improve SIEM accuracy and detection capabilities.

The adoption of SIEM in SMEs is increasing as cybersecurity threats become more sophisticated and regulatory requirements become more stringent. With the rise of cloud-based SIEM solutions, smaller organizations can now access advanced security capabilities without the high costs and complexity traditionally associated with SIEM deployments. By leveraging SIEM for continuous threat monitoring, compliance automation, and incident response, SMEs can strengthen their security posture and protect their digital assets from cyber threats. As SIEM technology continues to evolve, its accessibility and usability for SMEs will improve further, enabling smaller organizations to implement enterprise-grade security solutions tailored to their needs.

Cloud-Native SIEM Solutions

Cloud-native SIEM solutions are transforming the way organizations manage security by providing scalable, flexible, and efficient security monitoring in modern cloud environments. Traditional SIEM systems were originally designed for on-premises infrastructures, relying on hardware-based storage and manual configurations to collect and analyze security logs. However, as organizations increasingly migrate to cloud platforms such as Amazon Web Services (AWS), Microsoft Azure, and Google Cloud Platform (GCP), traditional SIEM solutions often struggle to keep pace with the scale and complexity of cloud-native applications, services, and workloads. Cloud-native SIEM solutions are specifically designed to address these challenges, offering real-time security monitoring, automated threat detection, and seamless integration with cloud services without the need for extensive infrastructure management.

One of the defining characteristics of cloud-native SIEM solutions is their ability to scale dynamically based on demand. Unlike traditional SIEM systems that require organizations to provision and maintain on-premises servers, cloud-native SIEM operates in a fully managed, serverless environment. This means that organizations do not need to worry about hardware limitations, storage capacity, or system upgrades. Cloud-native SIEM platforms automatically adjust their processing power and storage based on log ingestion rates, ensuring that security monitoring remains efficient even as an organization's IT infrastructure grows. This scalability makes cloud-native SIEM particularly beneficial for businesses that experience fluctuations in data volume, such as e-commerce companies during peak shopping seasons or financial institutions handling increased transactions.

Real-time log ingestion and analysis are critical components of cloud-native SIEM solutions. Traditional SIEM systems often process logs in batches, leading to delays in detecting security incidents. Cloud-native SIEM platforms leverage real-time data streaming technologies to collect, normalize, and analyze security events as they occur. This enables security teams to detect threats immediately and respond faster to potential incidents. By integrating with cloud services through API-based log collection, cloud-native SIEM platforms provide continuous visibility into user activity, network traffic, and application behavior across multi-cloud environments.

The integration of machine learning and artificial intelligence enhances the detection capabilities of cloud-native SIEM. Traditional SIEM solutions rely on predefined correlation rules to identify threats, but these rules require constant updates and may fail to detect new attack techniques. Machine learning-driven SIEM solutions analyze historical security data to identify behavioral patterns and detect anomalies that may indicate cyber threats. AI-driven threat detection reduces false positives by distinguishing between normal variations in activity and genuine security risks. User and Entity Behavior Analytics (UEBA) further strengthens threat detection by continuously monitoring user actions, privilege escalations, and access patterns, identifying potential insider threats or compromised accounts.

Automation plays a significant role in cloud-native SIEM solutions by streamlining incident response and reducing the workload on security analysts. Traditional SIEM systems often require manual investigation and remediation of security incidents, leading to delays in response time. Cloud-native SIEM integrates with Security Orchestration, Automation, and Response (SOAR) platforms to automate threat mitigation workflows. When a security event is detected, automated response actions can be triggered, such as isolating a compromised virtual machine, revoking access to suspicious user accounts, or blocking malicious IP addresses. This level of automation minimizes human intervention, allowing security teams to focus on more complex threat investigations while ensuring that critical threats are addressed immediately.

Threat intelligence integration is another key advantage of cloud-native SIEM. Cyber threats evolve rapidly, and organizations need up-to-date threat intelligence to defend against emerging attacks. Cloud-native SIEM solutions incorporate real-time threat intelligence feeds from global cybersecurity research groups, government agencies, and commercial threat intelligence providers. By correlating internal security events with external threat intelligence data, cloud-native SIEM platforms help security teams prioritize high-risk incidents and proactively defend against known attack patterns. Automated threat enrichment provides analysts with context about detected threats, including attacker tactics, techniques, and procedures, improving incident investigation and response.

Compliance monitoring and reporting are simplified with cloud-native SIEM solutions. Many industries are subject to stringent regulatory requirements that mandate security log retention, access monitoring, and audit reporting. Cloud-native SIEM platforms provide built-in compliance management features, automating the collection and storage of security logs required for regulations such as GDPR, HIPAA, PCI DSS, and ISO 27001. These platforms generate compliance reports with minimal manual effort, helping organizations demonstrate adherence to security policies and regulatory standards. Cloud-native SIEM also ensures that security logs are stored securely in geographically distributed data centers, reducing the risk of data loss and ensuring compliance with data sovereignty laws.

The flexibility of cloud-native SIEM extends to its ability to support hybrid and multi-cloud environments. Many organizations operate in hybrid infrastructures, combining on-premises data centers with cloud-based workloads. Cloud-native SIEM platforms integrate with both traditional IT systems and modern cloud environments, providing a unified security monitoring solution across all assets. By aggregating security logs from on-premises servers, virtual machines, containers, and cloud services, cloud-native SIEM solutions offer comprehensive visibility into the entire attack surface. Security teams can use a centralized dashboard to monitor security events across multiple cloud providers, reducing complexity and improving threat correlation.

Cost efficiency is a major advantage of cloud-native SIEM compared to traditional deployments. On-premises SIEM solutions require significant upfront investment in hardware, licensing, and maintenance. In contrast, cloud-native SIEM operates on a subscription-based or pay-as-you-go pricing model, allowing organizations to pay only for the resources they consume. This cost-effective approach is particularly beneficial for small and medium enterprises (SMEs) that may not have the budget for a fully on-premises security infrastructure. Cloud-native SIEM eliminates the need for dedicated security hardware, reducing operational costs while providing enterprise-grade security capabilities.

Despite its many benefits, organizations implementing cloud-native SIEM must consider potential challenges such as data privacy concerns, integration complexity, and visibility gaps. Some organizations may have concerns about storing security logs in a public cloud environment, particularly in industries with strict data privacy regulations. To address this, cloud-native SIEM vendors offer data encryption, role-based access controls, and the ability to store logs in specific geographic regions to comply with local regulations. Additionally, integrating cloud-native SIEM with legacy IT systems may require careful planning to ensure seamless log collection across different environments. Organizations should also implement continuous monitoring strategies to address any blind spots in cloud security visibility.

The adoption of cloud-native SIEM solutions is increasing as organizations recognize the need for scalable, efficient, and automated security monitoring. By leveraging real-time log processing, machine learning-driven analytics, automated incident response, and threat intelligence integration, cloud-native SIEM platforms enhance an organization's ability to detect and respond to cyber threats in dynamic IT environments. As cloud computing continues to grow, SIEM technology will continue to evolve, offering even more advanced capabilities to secure modern cloud infrastructures while providing organizations with the agility and efficiency required to defend against evolving cyber threats.

The Impact of Zero Trust on SIEM Design

The Zero Trust security model has significantly influenced the design and functionality of Security Information and Event Management (SIEM) systems. Traditionally, SIEM solutions were designed around perimeter-based security, which assumes that internal networks are inherently trusted while external traffic is considered potentially malicious. However, as cyber threats have evolved and remote work, cloud adoption, and supply chain attacks have increased, the perimeter-based model has become obsolete. Zero Trust operates on the principle of never assuming trust, requiring continuous verification of all users, devices, and applications, regardless of whether they are inside or outside the network. This shift in security philosophy has forced SIEM systems to evolve, integrating identity-centric security monitoring, real-time risk assessments, and more granular policy enforcement mechanisms.

One of the fundamental changes that Zero Trust brings to SIEM design is the focus on identity and access management (IAM). Traditional SIEM solutions primarily monitored network traffic, firewall logs, and endpoint activity to detect threats. However, Zero Trust prioritizes identity as the primary security control, requiring SIEM systems to deeply integrate with IAM solutions, multifactor authentication (MFA), and privileged access management (PAM) tools. SIEM platforms now need to analyze user behaviors, monitor access requests, and correlate identity-related events with security incidents. If a user attempts to access a sensitive application from an unfamiliar location or device, SIEM can trigger alerts, flagging the activity as a potential security risk. This identity-centric approach ensures that unauthorized access attempts are detected and mitigated in real time.

Behavioral analytics plays a critical role in aligning SIEM with Zero Trust principles. Since Zero Trust assumes that attackers could already be inside the network, SIEM solutions must continuously monitor user and device behavior to identify anomalies. Machine learning-driven User and Entity Behavior Analytics (UEBA) enhances SIEM capabilities by detecting deviations from normal activity. If a user typically logs in from a corporate office and suddenly accesses critical systems from an unknown geographic location, UEBA can flag this behavior as suspicious. Similarly, if an endpoint that normally interacts with specific servers begins communicating with unauthorized systems, SIEM can trigger an investigation. This continuous monitoring approach ensures that potential threats are detected before they escalate.

The integration of Zero Trust Network Access (ZTNA) with SIEM has redefined how security teams analyze network traffic and endpoint activity. Traditional network monitoring in SIEM focused on detecting anomalies in internal network traffic and perimeter defenses. With Zero Trust, network security shifts towards micro-segmentation, where access to resources is granted based on user identity, device security posture, and contextual risk factors. SIEM systems must now analyze access control policies, enforce least-privilege access, and correlate security logs from ZTNA solutions. Instead of relying solely on firewall rules, SIEM must evaluate whether a user's access request aligns with predefined security policies and risk levels. If an unauthorized user attempts to access a restricted segment, SIEM can generate alerts and trigger automated responses to block access.

Endpoint visibility is another area where Zero Trust has transformed SIEM requirements. Traditional SIEM implementations primarily focused on detecting malware infections and unauthorized system changes based on predefined signatures. Zero Trust requires SIEM to continuously monitor endpoint compliance, device health, and security posture. By integrating with Endpoint Detection and Response

(EDR) solutions, SIEM can detect compromised endpoints, identify unpatched vulnerabilities, and enforce Zero Trust security policies. If an endpoint fails a security compliance check, SIEM can trigger remediation actions, such as revoking access to sensitive systems or isolating the device from the network. This proactive approach reduces the attack surface and prevents compromised endpoints from becoming entry points for cybercriminals.

Cloud security monitoring has become a key component of SIEM in a Zero Trust environment. As organizations shift workloads to cloud platforms, security perimeters become more fluid, making traditional network-based monitoring ineffective. SIEM systems must now integrate with cloud access security brokers (CASBs), cloud-native security tools, and identity-based access controls to provide comprehensive security visibility. Instead of assuming that cloud workloads are secure by default, SIEM must continuously analyze cloud access logs, detect misconfigurations, and enforce Zero Trust principles in multi-cloud environments. If a cloud administrator grants excessive privileges to a user or an application attempts to access unauthorized resources, SIEM can generate alerts and enforce security controls.

Automated incident response is crucial in SIEM's adaptation to Zero Trust. Since Zero Trust assumes that threats can emerge from anywhere, real-time response mechanisms are necessary to contain security incidents before they cause damage. SIEM solutions now integrate with Security Orchestration, Automation, and Response (SOAR) platforms to enforce Zero Trust policies automatically. If a user's behavior indicates potential credential compromise, SIEM can trigger automated responses such as requiring MFA, revoking session tokens, or quarantining the affected user account. This automated approach reduces response time, minimizes the impact of security incidents, and ensures that security policies are enforced consistently.

Threat intelligence integration enhances SIEM's effectiveness in a Zero Trust framework. Modern SIEM platforms incorporate real-time threat intelligence feeds that provide information about known attack vectors, malicious IP addresses, and emerging cyber threats. Zero Trust requires continuous risk assessment, meaning SIEM must correlate security events with external threat intelligence to determine if an access request, login attempt, or network connection aligns with known threat patterns. If an employee's credentials appear on a leaked credential database or if an endpoint communicates with a known command-and-control server, SIEM can immediately block access and initiate threat mitigation workflows.

Zero Trust's emphasis on continuous authentication has also influenced SIEM's approach to compliance monitoring. Many regulatory frameworks, including GDPR, HIPAA, PCI DSS, and NIST, require organizations to implement strong access controls and maintain audit logs of all security events. SIEM solutions now play a central role in ensuring compliance by tracking authentication attempts, failed logins, and unauthorized access attempts. Automated compliance reporting helps organizations demonstrate adherence to Zero Trust security models while providing auditors with detailed visibility into access control policies and enforcement mechanisms.

The shift towards Zero Trust has also redefined how SIEM systems handle log aggregation and correlation. Traditional SIEM solutions primarily collected logs from on-premises network appliances, but Zero Trust requires the collection and analysis of security data from diverse sources, including cloud services, identity providers, endpoint security platforms, and third-party applications. SIEM systems must now ingest and correlate data across these distributed environments, ensuring that security teams have a unified view of potential threats. This distributed logging approach enhances security visibility and ensures that SIEM can detect threats across hybrid IT ecosystems.

Zero Trust has fundamentally reshaped SIEM design by shifting the focus from perimeter-based security to identity-centric, behavior-driven threat detection. Modern SIEM solutions must continuously verify users, enforce least-privilege access, analyze behavioral patterns, and automate threat responses. The integration of Zero Trust principles into SIEM enhances security visibility, reduces the attack surface, and ensures that security teams can detect and mitigate threats in real time. As organizations continue to adopt Zero Trust architectures, SIEM will remain a critical component in enforcing security policies, protecting sensitive data, and preventing unauthorized access across dynamic IT environments.

Managed SIEM vs. On-Premises SIEM

Organizations implementing a Security Information and Event Management (SIEM) solution must decide between a managed SIEM service and an on-premises SIEM deployment. Each approach offers distinct advantages and challenges, making it essential to align the choice with an organization's security needs, IT resources, budget, and operational requirements. Managed SIEM services provide outsourced security monitoring and management, allowing organizations to leverage the expertise of a third-party provider. On-premises SIEM solutions, on the other hand, require in-house deployment, maintenance, and administration but offer complete control over security data and configurations. The decision between managed and on-premises SIEM significantly impacts an organization's ability to detect threats, respond to incidents, and maintain compliance with regulatory requirements.

One of the primary factors influencing the choice between managed SIEM and on-premises SIEM is resource availability. Deploying an on-premises SIEM solution requires significant investment in hardware, software licensing, and skilled personnel to manage and maintain the system. Organizations must configure log sources, develop correlation rules, fine-tune alerts, and conduct regular system updates to ensure optimal performance. This level of commitment can be challenging for businesses with small IT teams or limited cybersecurity expertise. Managed SIEM services address this issue by providing a fully outsourced solution, where security analysts, engineers, and threat intelligence specialists handle monitoring, tuning, and incident response. This allows organizations to benefit from SIEM capabilities without the need for extensive in-house security expertise.

Scalability is another critical consideration when comparing managed SIEM and on-premises SIEM. As organizations grow, the volume of security logs and events increases, requiring greater processing power and storage capacity. Scaling an on-premises SIEM system involves upgrading hardware, increasing storage, and optimizing system performance to accommodate higher log ingestion rates. This process can be costly and time-consuming. Managed SIEM services offer a more scalable approach by leveraging cloud-based infrastructures that automatically adjust to increasing data volumes. Organizations using managed SIEM can scale security monitoring without worrying about infrastructure limitations, making it an attractive option for businesses with dynamic security needs.

Cost is a major factor in the SIEM selection process. On-premises SIEM solutions require substantial upfront investment in hardware, software, and personnel. Ongoing costs include system maintenance, updates, and the salaries of security analysts required to manage the SIEM system effectively. In contrast, managed SIEM services operate on a subscription-based pricing model, allowing organizations to pay for security monitoring as a service rather than investing in infrastructure. This predictable cost structure makes managed SIEM more accessible to small and medium-sized businesses that lack the budget for a full-scale on-premises SIEM deployment. However, organizations with long-term security needs may find that an on-premises SIEM provides greater cost efficiency over time, as they avoid recurring subscription fees associated with managed SIEM services.

Threat detection and response capabilities vary between managed SIEM and on-premises SIEM deployments. On-premises SIEM solutions provide full control over security policies, correlation rules, and alert configurations. Organizations can customize threat detection mechanisms to align with their specific risk profiles and industry requirements. Security teams have direct access to logs and can conduct in-depth forensic investigations without relying on external service providers. Managed SIEM services, while offering robust threat detection, operate with predefined monitoring rules and correlation logic. Although managed SIEM providers continuously update detection algorithms based on global threat intelligence, organizations may have less flexibility to customize detection rules tailored to their unique security environment.

Incident response efficiency is another key differentiator between managed SIEM and on-premises SIEM. On-premises SIEM solutions provide direct access to security event logs, enabling internal security teams to investigate incidents immediately. This hands-on approach allows organizations to respond quickly to security threats, provided they have a dedicated security operations team. Managed SIEM services, on the other hand, rely on third-party analysts to triage alerts and escalate critical incidents. While this outsourcing model ensures round-the-clock security monitoring, response times may be affected by communication delays between the managed SIEM provider and the organization's internal IT team. Some managed SIEM services include automated response actions, such as blocking malicious IP addresses or disabling compromised user accounts, but organizations must establish clear response workflows to avoid delays in threat mitigation.

Data privacy and compliance considerations play a crucial role in SIEM deployment decisions. On-premises SIEM solutions give organizations full control over security logs, ensuring that sensitive data remains within their internal infrastructure. This is particularly important for industries with strict regulatory requirements, such as healthcare, finance, and government, where organizations must comply with data residency laws and maintain complete visibility into security logs. Managed SIEM services, which often operate in cloud environments, may introduce challenges related to data sovereignty, regulatory compliance, and third-party access to security data. Organizations must carefully assess managed SIEM providers' data handling policies, encryption mechanisms, and compliance certifications to ensure that security logs are protected and meet regulatory standards.

Customization and integration capabilities differ significantly between managed SIEM and on-premises SIEM. On-premises SIEM solutions allow organizations to integrate security monitoring with existing IT and security tools, including identity and access management (IAM), endpoint detection and response (EDR), and security automation platforms. Custom dashboards, reporting, and correlation rules can be tailored to align with the organization's security strategy. Managed SIEM services, while offering integration with popular security platforms, may have limitations in customization. Organizations relying on industry-specific security frameworks or proprietary systems may find that an on-premises SIEM provides greater flexibility in integrating with their existing security infrastructure.

Time to deployment is another factor that organizations must consider. Implementing an on-premises SIEM solution requires careful planning, log source configuration, correlation rule development, and extensive testing before the system becomes fully operational. This deployment process can take weeks or even months, depending on the complexity of the IT environment. Managed SIEM services offer faster deployment times, as they are preconfigured and optimized by the service provider. Organizations can start monitoring security events almost immediately after onboarding with a managed SIEM provider, making it a more efficient option for businesses that need rapid security visibility.

Choosing between managed SIEM and on-premises SIEM ultimately depends on an organization's security maturity, resource availability, compliance requirements, and operational needs. Managed SIEM is an ideal choice for organizations seeking a cost-effective, scalable, and outsourced security monitoring solution that provides 24/7 threat detection without requiring extensive internal security expertise. On-premises SIEM is best suited for organizations that require complete control over security data, customized detection rules, and integration with proprietary security tools. By carefully evaluating the advantages and limitations of each approach, organizations can select the SIEM deployment model that best aligns with their cybersecurity objectives and long-term security strategy.

SIEM for Industrial Control Systems (ICS)

Security Information and Event Management (SIEM) solutions play a crucial role in protecting Industrial Control Systems (ICS) from cyber threats, operational disruptions, and security incidents. Industrial environments, including power plants, manufacturing facilities, oil refineries, and water treatment plants, rely on ICS to manage critical infrastructure. Unlike traditional IT environments, ICS operates with specialized hardware and software, such as Supervisory Control and Data Acquisition (SCADA) systems, Programmable Logic Controllers (PLCs), and Distributed Control Systems (DCS). These systems were originally designed with a focus on reliability and uptime rather than security, making them vulnerable to cyberattacks, insider threats, and operational failures. The integration of SIEM in ICS environments provides enhanced visibility, real-time threat detection, and incident response capabilities to safeguard industrial processes.

One of the key challenges in securing ICS is the convergence of IT and Operational Technology (OT). Traditionally, ICS operated in isolated environments with minimal connectivity to external networks.

However, the adoption of industrial IoT (IIoT), remote monitoring, and cloud-based analytics has increased the exposure of ICS to cyber threats. SIEM solutions help bridge the gap between IT and OT security by aggregating logs from both environments, correlating security events, and identifying anomalies that could indicate a cyberattack. By providing a unified view of security incidents across IT and OT infrastructures, SIEM enhances situational awareness and helps security teams detect threats before they impact industrial operations.

ICS environments generate vast amounts of operational data, including sensor readings, process logs, and control commands. Unlike traditional IT networks, where log collection focuses on user authentication, firewall activity, and endpoint security, ICS log sources include SCADA logs, PLC event records, and network traffic between industrial devices. SIEM solutions tailored for ICS must be capable of ingesting and analyzing these specialized log sources while distinguishing between normal operational behavior and potential security threats. Advanced SIEM systems incorporate machine learning and behavioral analytics to establish baselines of normal ICS activity, enabling the detection of deviations that could indicate a cyberattack, unauthorized access, or system malfunction.

Real-time threat detection is essential in ICS environments, where operational disruptions can have severe consequences, including financial losses, environmental damage, and threats to public safety. Traditional SIEM solutions rely on predefined correlation rules to identify security incidents, but ICS threats often involve subtle, gradual changes in system behavior rather than clear indicators of compromise. SIEM for ICS integrates anomaly detection techniques that analyze process variables, network communication patterns, and user behavior to identify suspicious activity. If a PLC begins receiving unauthorized commands or a SCADA workstation initiates an unexpected connection to an external IP address, the SIEM system can generate alerts for immediate investigation.

The integration of SIEM with Industrial Intrusion Detection Systems (IDS) strengthens security monitoring for ICS environments. Unlike IT-focused IDS solutions that analyze signature-based attack patterns, industrial IDS solutions monitor control protocols such as Modbus, DNP3, and OPC UA for unauthorized or anomalous activity. SIEM platforms correlate industrial IDS alerts with logs from firewalls, authentication systems, and network traffic analysis tools to provide a comprehensive view of security threats. By aggregating data from multiple sources, SIEM enhances the accuracy of threat detection and reduces false positives, ensuring that security teams focus on genuine threats rather than operational noise.

Incident response in ICS environments requires a delicate balance between security and operational continuity. Unlike IT systems, where security incidents can often be mitigated through patching, software updates, or system reboots, ICS downtime can disrupt critical industrial processes. SIEM solutions support automated response actions tailored for ICS environments, such as isolating compromised network segments, restricting unauthorized commands, and alerting industrial operators to potential security breaches. Security Orchestration, Automation, and Response (SOAR) integration enables SIEM to trigger predefined incident response workflows, ensuring that security teams can contain threats without causing unnecessary disruptions to industrial operations.

Regulatory compliance is a significant driver for SIEM adoption in ICS environments. Many industries that rely on ICS are subject to strict cybersecurity regulations, including NERC CIP for the energy sector, IEC 62443 for industrial automation, and the NIST Cybersecurity Framework for critical infrastructure. These regulations require organizations to implement continuous monitoring, log retention, and incident reporting mechanisms to ensure the security and resilience of industrial operations. SIEM solutions automate compliance reporting by collecting security event data, generating audit logs, and ensuring that organizations meet regulatory requirements. By streamlining compliance management, SIEM reduces the administrative burden on industrial security teams while improving overall security posture.

Insider threats pose a significant risk to ICS environments, where unauthorized modifications to control systems can lead to catastrophic failures. Unlike traditional cybersecurity threats that originate from external attackers, insider threats involve employees, contractors, or third-party vendors with legitimate access to industrial networks. SIEM solutions enhance insider threat detection by monitoring privileged user activity, tracking administrative actions on control systems, and identifying deviations from normal operational behavior. If a user attempts to modify critical PLC configurations outside of authorized maintenance windows or accesses sensitive control system files without prior approval, SIEM can generate alerts for security personnel to investigate.

Supply chain security is another growing concern for ICS operators, as industrial environments increasingly rely on third-party vendors, remote maintenance services, and cloud-based analytics platforms. Compromised third-party software, unpatched vulnerabilities in industrial devices, and malicious firmware updates can introduce security risks to ICS networks. SIEM solutions provide supply chain visibility by monitoring software updates, verifying digital signatures of industrial applications, and detecting unauthorized access from external service providers. By correlating security events across internal and external sources, SIEM helps organizations identify potential supply chain attacks and take proactive measures to mitigate risks.

The evolution of SIEM in ICS environments is driven by advancements in artificial intelligence, machine learning, and predictive analytics. Traditional SIEM implementations relied on historical log analysis to detect security incidents after they occurred. Modern SIEM solutions incorporate predictive security analytics, enabling organizations to anticipate threats before they impact industrial operations. By analyzing trends in system behavior, correlating threat intelligence feeds, and applying AI-driven risk assessments, SIEM can identify early warning signs of cyber threats and provide actionable insights to security teams. This proactive approach enhances the resilience of ICS environments against both known and emerging cyber risks.

The deployment of SIEM in ICS environments presents unique challenges, including the need for specialized security expertise, integration with legacy industrial systems, and the potential for operational disruptions during implementation. Many ICS environments operate with legacy control systems that lack built-in security features or logging capabilities. SIEM deployment in such environments requires careful planning to ensure that security monitoring does not interfere with industrial processes. Organizations must work closely with both IT and OT teams to implement SIEM in a way that enhances security without compromising system availability.

SIEM has become an essential component of cybersecurity strategies for industrial control systems, providing real-time monitoring, threat detection, and compliance enforcement. By integrating with industrial security tools, leveraging behavioral analytics, and automating incident response, SIEM helps ICS operators protect critical infrastructure from cyber threats. As ICS environments continue to evolve with the adoption of digital transformation, cloud-based monitoring, and industrial IoT, SIEM solutions will play an increasingly vital role in securing industrial operations and ensuring the reliability of essential services.

Implementing SIEM for Compliance Audits

Security Information and Event Management (SIEM) solutions play a critical role in helping organizations meet regulatory requirements and successfully complete compliance audits. Regulatory frameworks such as GDPR, HIPAA, PCI DSS, ISO 27001, and NIST mandate strict security controls, log retention policies, and continuous monitoring of security events. SIEM provides organizations with the ability to collect, analyze, and retain security logs, ensuring that they maintain compliance with industry regulations and are prepared for audit requirements. By automating compliance monitoring and reporting, SIEM reduces the administrative burden on security teams while improving visibility into security risks. Implementing SIEM effectively for compliance audits requires proper configuration, integration with relevant log sources, and the ability to generate audit-ready reports that demonstrate adherence to security policies.

One of the primary reasons organizations implement SIEM for compliance is the need for continuous log monitoring. Regulatory standards require organizations to maintain detailed records of system access, user activities, authentication attempts, and security events. SIEM systems centralize log collection from multiple sources, including firewalls, intrusion detection systems (IDS), antivirus software, cloud services, and endpoint devices. By aggregating these logs into a single platform, SIEM provides auditors with a comprehensive view of security events, helping organizations demonstrate that they have effective monitoring mechanisms in place. The ability to correlate security events across different log sources allows organizations to detect potential compliance violations and address security gaps before they become audit findings.

Log retention is a key compliance requirement that varies depending on the regulatory framework. For example, PCI DSS mandates that organizations retain security logs for at least one year, with the most recent three months readily available for immediate analysis. Similarly, HIPAA requires healthcare organizations to maintain security logs for six years to ensure auditability and regulatory compliance. SIEM solutions automate log retention policies by storing logs securely, ensuring that they are tamper-proof, and enabling organizations to retrieve historical logs when needed. Advanced SIEM platforms also provide data integrity mechanisms, such as digital signatures and encryption, to ensure that stored logs cannot be modified or deleted without authorization.

Automated reporting is another major advantage of using SIEM for compliance audits. Preparing audit reports manually can be time-consuming and error-prone, particularly for organizations with complex IT environments. SIEM systems streamline the reporting process by generating compliance-specific reports that align with regulatory requirements. These reports summarize key security metrics, such as failed login attempts, privilege escalations, unauthorized access attempts, and suspicious activities. Organizations can configure SIEM dashboards to track compliance status in real time, ensuring that they are continuously meeting regulatory obligations. When auditors request documentation, SIEM enables security teams to generate audit-ready reports instantly, reducing the time and effort required to prepare for compliance assessments.

Access control monitoring is a fundamental aspect of compliance audits, as most regulations require organizations to enforce strict user authentication and privilege management policies. SIEM enhances access control monitoring by tracking user authentication logs, login failures, privilege escalations, and account modifications. If an employee attempts to access restricted systems without proper authorization, SIEM generates alerts and logs the activity for compliance review. Organizations can use SIEM to enforce role-based access controls (RBAC), ensuring that only authorized personnel have access to sensitive data and critical systems. By correlating access logs with security events, SIEM helps organizations identify insider threats, unauthorized data access, and policy violations.

Threat detection and incident response are integral to compliance requirements, particularly in frameworks that mandate timely reporting of security incidents. For example, GDPR requires organizations to report data breaches within 72 hours, while HIPAA mandates that covered entities notify affected individuals and regulatory authorities within a specific timeframe. SIEM facilitates compliance by providing real-time threat detection and automated incident response capabilities. When a security event occurs, SIEM generates alerts, escalates incidents to security teams, and documents response actions for audit purposes. The ability to demonstrate that an organization has an effective incident response process in place is crucial for passing compliance audits and avoiding regulatory penalties.

Fraud detection and financial transaction monitoring are particularly important for industries subject to financial regulations such as SOX (Sarbanes-Oxley Act) and PCI DSS. SIEM helps financial institutions and payment processors monitor financial transactions for signs of fraud, account takeovers, and payment card data exposure. By analyzing transaction logs and detecting deviations from normal patterns, SIEM can flag suspicious activities such as multiple failed payment attempts, unusual transaction volumes, or unauthorized changes to financial records. Compliance auditors require organizations to prove that they have implemented fraud detection mechanisms, and SIEM provides the necessary visibility and reporting to meet these requirements.

SIEM also enhances supply chain security compliance by monitoring third-party access to critical systems and data. Many regulatory frameworks, such as the NIST Cybersecurity Framework, require organizations to assess the security practices of vendors and contractors who have access to their IT infrastructure. SIEM enables organizations to track third-party logins, monitor data transfers involving external entities, and detect unauthorized access attempts from vendors. If a third-party system shows signs of compromise, SIEM can generate alerts and trigger response actions to prevent further exposure. The ability to demonstrate strong supply chain security practices is increasingly important for passing compliance audits and mitigating risks associated with third-party access.

Encryption and data protection requirements are another focus area for compliance audits. Regulations such as GDPR and CCPA mandate that organizations implement encryption to protect sensitive customer data. SIEM helps organizations ensure compliance by monitoring encryption policies, identifying unencrypted data transfers, and detecting vulnerabilities in data protection mechanisms. By logging encryption status and security certificate usage, SIEM provides auditors with verifiable records that demonstrate adherence to data protection regulations. Organizations that fail to enforce encryption policies may face regulatory fines, making SIEM an essential tool for monitoring data security practices.

Continuous compliance monitoring is a growing trend in regulatory frameworks, requiring organizations to maintain security controls at all times rather than conducting periodic compliance checks. SIEM solutions support continuous compliance by integrating real-time monitoring, automated log analysis, and proactive threat detection. Instead of treating compliance as a one-time audit exercise, organizations can use SIEM to enforce security policies, detect violations, and remediate compliance issues before they escalate. By leveraging SIEM for continuous compliance monitoring, organizations reduce the risk of audit failures and improve their ability to respond to evolving regulatory requirements.

The implementation of SIEM for compliance audits requires careful planning, proper log source integration, and ongoing fine-tuning of security policies. Organizations must ensure that all relevant security logs are collected, retention policies align with regulatory mandates, and reporting capabilities are configured to generate accurate audit documentation. By using SIEM as a centralized compliance management tool, organizations can streamline audit processes, reduce manual reporting efforts, and improve their overall security posture. As regulatory requirements continue to evolve, SIEM remains a critical asset for organizations seeking to maintain compliance, protect sensitive data, and demonstrate accountability in security operations.

Cost Considerations in SIEM Deployment

Deploying a Security Information and Event Management (SIEM) system requires careful cost analysis to ensure that an organization achieves the best return on investment while maintaining effective security monitoring. SIEM solutions vary in pricing depending on factors such as deployment model, log volume, licensing structure, and required integrations. Organizations must evaluate the total cost of ownership (TCO), including upfront expenses, ongoing maintenance, personnel costs, and potential hidden fees. A well-planned SIEM deployment balances security needs with financial constraints, ensuring that the organization receives maximum value without unnecessary expenditures.

One of the primary cost factors in SIEM deployment is the choice between on-premises and cloud-based solutions. On-premises SIEM requires significant upfront investment in hardware, software licenses, and storage capacity. Organizations must purchase and maintain physical servers, networking equipment, and storage systems to handle log ingestion and retention. These infrastructure costs can be substantial, particularly for large enterprises that generate high volumes of security logs. Additionally, on-premises SIEM requires dedicated personnel to manage configurations, perform software updates, and optimize performance. While on-premises deployments provide complete control over security data, they come with long-term operational costs, including power consumption, hardware upgrades, and system monitoring.

Cloud-based SIEM solutions offer a more flexible and scalable pricing model, typically following a subscription-based structure. Instead of investing in physical infrastructure, organizations pay for cloud-based SIEM as a service, with costs determined by log volume, data retention duration, and the number of monitored assets. This model eliminates the need for hardware purchases and reduces maintenance expenses, making it an attractive option for organizations looking to minimize capital expenditures. However, cloud-based SIEM pricing can become complex due to variable costs associated with data ingestion, API usage, and additional security features such as advanced analytics and machine learning-driven threat detection. Organizations must carefully evaluate cloud SIEM pricing tiers to avoid unexpected expenses.

Log volume is another significant cost driver in SIEM deployment. SIEM systems collect logs from multiple sources, including firewalls, endpoint security tools, authentication servers, cloud services, and network traffic analysis platforms. Many SIEM vendors price their solutions based on the volume of logs ingested daily, measured in gigabytes or events per second (EPS). Organizations with high log generation rates may face escalating costs, particularly if they retain logs for extended periods. To optimize costs, organizations should implement log filtering strategies that prioritize critical security events while reducing unnecessary data ingestion. By defining which logs are essential for security monitoring and compliance, organizations can control SIEM costs without sacrificing threat detection capabilities.

Data retention policies impact the long-term cost of SIEM deployment. Compliance requirements often mandate that organizations retain security logs for extended periods, ranging from several months to multiple years. Retaining large volumes of log data requires substantial storage resources, whether on-premises or in the cloud. Organizations must evaluate the cost implications of long-term storage, including data archiving solutions, compression techniques, and tiered storage options. Some SIEM vendors offer cold storage options that reduce costs by moving older logs to lower-cost storage tiers while keeping recent logs readily accessible for real-time analysis. Balancing compliance requirements with storage costs is crucial to maintaining an efficient and cost-effective SIEM deployment.

Licensing models also influence SIEM deployment costs. Vendors offer various licensing structures, including perpetual licenses, subscription-based pricing, and usage-based billing. Perpetual licensing involves a one-time purchase of SIEM software, with additional costs for annual maintenance, support, and upgrades. This model is common for on-premises deployments but requires a higher initial investment. Subscription-based pricing, often used in cloud SIEM, allows organizations to pay a recurring fee based on usage metrics such as data ingestion, user count, or asset coverage. While subscription-based models provide cost flexibility, organizations must monitor their usage to prevent exceeding allocated limits, which can lead to additional charges. Usage-based billing models charge organizations based on actual log consumption, providing scalability but requiring careful cost tracking to avoid budget overruns.

The cost of skilled personnel is a critical factor in SIEM deployment. Effective SIEM management requires experienced security analysts, engineers, and administrators to configure correlation rules, investigate alerts, and fine-tune detection mechanisms. Hiring and retaining qualified cybersecurity professionals can be expensive, particularly in organizations with limited security expertise. Managed SIEM services provide an alternative by outsourcing SIEM monitoring and management to third-party providers. While managed SIEM reduces personnel costs, organizations must factor in service fees and ensure that response times align with their security needs. Whether using an in-house team or a managed service provider, organizations must account for training, certifications, and continuous skill development to maximize the effectiveness of their SIEM investment.

Integration with existing security tools and IT infrastructure adds another layer of costs to SIEM deployment. SIEM systems must seamlessly integrate with firewalls, intrusion detection systems (IDS), endpoint detection and response (EDR) platforms, and cloud security solutions. Some SIEM vendors offer native integrations at no additional cost, while others require separate licensing for third-party connectors and API usage. Custom integrations may involve development costs, requiring organizations to invest in scripting, automation, and API management. Evaluating integration costs before deployment ensures that SIEM solutions can work efficiently with existing security tools without exceeding budgetary constraints.

Performance optimization and scalability considerations also affect SIEM costs. Organizations must ensure that their SIEM solution can handle growing log volumes, evolving threat landscapes, and increased security monitoring requirements over time. Scaling an on-premises SIEM system requires additional hardware investment, whereas cloud SIEM solutions allow for on-demand scalability. However, cloud-based scalability often comes with increased costs based on usage spikes. Organizations should implement cost control measures such as dynamic log retention, resource optimization, and predictive analytics to ensure that SIEM remains cost-effective as security needs expand.

Compliance and regulatory requirements further influence SIEM costs. Many industries require organizations to conduct security audits, generate compliance reports, and maintain audit logs for regulatory purposes. SIEM solutions with built-in compliance automation reduce manual efforts but may come with additional licensing fees for compliance-specific features. Organizations should assess whether compliance reporting is included in the base SIEM package or requires a premium subscription. Investing in SIEM solutions with automated compliance reporting capabilities can help organizations save time and reduce the risk of regulatory fines.

Organizations deploying SIEM must also consider potential hidden costs, including software updates, vendor support fees, and incident response costs. SIEM platforms require continuous updates to maintain detection accuracy, integrate new threat intelligence feeds, and improve system performance. Some vendors charge additional fees for premium support, faster response times, or advanced security analytics features. Additionally, organizations must account for the indirect costs of incident response, such as downtime, remediation efforts, and forensic investigations. Proper budgeting ensures that SIEM deployment costs align with long-term security objectives while minimizing unexpected financial burdens.

SIEM deployment costs vary widely depending on factors such as deployment model, log volume, licensing structure, personnel costs, and integration requirements. Organizations must conduct a thorough cost-benefit analysis to determine the most efficient and cost-effective SIEM solution for their security needs. By optimizing log ingestion, managing data retention, selecting the right licensing model, and considering managed service options, organizations can control SIEM costs while maintaining strong security monitoring capabilities. Strategic planning and continuous cost evaluation help ensure that SIEM remains a valuable investment in an organization's cybersecurity infrastructure without exceeding budgetary limitations.

The Future of Threat Hunting with SIEM

Threat hunting is evolving as cyber threats become more sophisticated, requiring organizations to move beyond traditional reactive security measures and adopt proactive detection strategies. Security Information and Event Management (SIEM) systems play a critical role in modern threat hunting by aggregating and analyzing vast amounts of security data to identify hidden threats before they can cause damage. The future of threat hunting with SIEM is being shaped by advancements in artificial intelligence, machine learning, automation, and deep behavioral analytics. As attackers continuously refine their tactics to bypass conventional security defenses, SIEM solutions must adapt to provide faster, more intelligent, and more automated threat hunting capabilities.

One of the most significant advancements in SIEM-driven threat hunting is the integration of artificial intelligence and machine learning. Traditional threat detection relies on predefined correlation rules and static indicators of compromise (IOCs), which are often ineffective against zero-day threats and advanced persistent threats (APTs). Machine learning models enable SIEM to detect anomalies based on deviations from normal behavior rather than relying solely on signature-based detection. By continuously analyzing user activities, network traffic patterns, and endpoint behaviors, SIEM systems can uncover subtle indicators of compromise that would otherwise go unnoticed. AI-powered threat hunting allows security teams to focus on investigating high-confidence threats while reducing the number of false positives generated by conventional detection methods.

Behavioral analytics is becoming an essential component of future SIEM-driven threat hunting. Instead of detecting threats based on known attack signatures, behavioral analytics identifies deviations in how users, applications, and systems typically operate. User and Entity Behavior Analytics (UEBA) enhances SIEM capabilities by establishing dynamic baselines for normal activity and flagging unusual patterns. If an employee who usually accesses internal resources during office hours suddenly attempts to transfer large volumes of data to an external cloud storage service at night, behavioral analytics will classify this as suspicious activity. By leveraging UEBA, SIEM solutions can detect insider threats, compromised credentials, and lateral movement within a network, providing security teams with deeper visibility into potential threats.

Automation is playing an increasingly important role in the future of threat hunting with SIEM. Manual threat-hunting processes require security analysts to sift through massive amounts of security logs, search for anomalies, and correlate different data points to identify threats. As cyberattacks become more complex, security teams cannot afford to rely solely on manual investigations. SIEM solutions are incorporating automation to streamline threat-hunting workflows, allowing analysts to perform searches, run queries, and correlate security events with minimal human intervention. Security Orchestration, Automation, and Response (SOAR) platforms integrated with SIEM help automate repetitive tasks, such as scanning for known threats, flagging suspicious behavior, and enriching security events with threat intelligence. This level of automation significantly reduces response times and allows security teams to focus on higher-priority investigations.

Threat intelligence integration is transforming how SIEM systems support proactive threat hunting. Modern SIEM platforms incorporate real-time threat intelligence feeds that provide updated information on emerging threats, known malicious IP addresses, malware signatures, and attacker tactics. By correlating internal security events with external threat intelligence, SIEM helps security teams identify new attack vectors and take preventive measures. Threat intelligence enrichment enables security analysts to determine the context behind security alerts, assess the risk level of detected threats, and prioritize response actions. Future SIEM solutions will leverage AI-driven threat intelligence analysis to predict emerging threats and automatically adjust detection rules based on evolving attack patterns.

The adoption of extended detection and response (XDR) is expanding SIEM's capabilities in threat hunting. Traditional SIEM systems primarily focus on aggregating logs and correlating security events from various sources. XDR extends this approach by integrating data from endpoints, cloud services, network security devices, and identity management solutions, creating a holistic view of security incidents. The convergence of SIEM and XDR enables security teams to conduct more comprehensive threat-hunting investigations, correlating endpoint activity with network anomalies and user behaviors. This integrated approach allows organizations to detect threats earlier in the attack lifecycle, improving the chances of mitigating security breaches before they escalate.

Predictive threat hunting is another emerging trend that will define the future of SIEM-driven security operations. Instead of responding to threats after they have been detected, predictive analytics uses historical security data to identify patterns that indicate potential attacks before they occur. By analyzing past security incidents, failed login attempts, lateral movement behaviors, and data exfiltration trends, SIEM can proactively alert security teams about possible attack attempts. AI-powered predictive threat hunting enables organizations to strengthen security defenses in advance, preventing attackers from exploiting vulnerabilities before they are identified through traditional security monitoring.

Cloud security monitoring is becoming an integral part of future SIEM-based threat hunting. As organizations move workloads to cloud platforms, traditional perimeter-based security measures are no longer sufficient to detect threats in highly distributed environments. SIEM solutions are evolving to provide deeper visibility into cloud activity, monitoring access logs, API usage, and anomalous behaviors within cloud-based applications. Future SIEM platforms will integrate seamlessly with cloud security tools, providing real-time threat detection across multi-cloud and hybrid environments. By leveraging cloud-native threat-hunting capabilities, organizations can detect and mitigate security risks in cloud workloads, containers, and serverless applications.

Threat hunting is also being enhanced by the use of proactive deception techniques. SIEM systems are incorporating honeypots, decoy accounts, and fake credentials to lure attackers into revealing their tactics. When an attacker interacts with a deception asset, SIEM generates an alert, providing security teams with early warning indicators of an intrusion attempt. Deception-based threat hunting allows organizations to gather intelligence on attacker methodologies, refine detection strategies, and improve response capabilities. Future SIEM platforms will integrate automated deception techniques to actively detect and disrupt cyber threats before they reach critical assets.

Collaboration between human analysts and AI-driven SIEM will define the next phase of threat hunting. While AI enhances detection accuracy and automates routine security tasks, human expertise remains essential for interpreting complex security incidents and making strategic decisions. Future SIEM solutions will incorporate AI-assisted threat-hunting interfaces, allowing security analysts to interact with machine learning models using natural language queries. Instead of manually searching through logs, analysts will be able to ask SIEM systems questions such as "Show me all login attempts from anomalous locations in the past 48 hours" and receive instant insights. This human-AI collaboration will make threat hunting more accessible and efficient for security teams of all skill levels.

As cyber threats continue to evolve, SIEM-driven threat hunting will become more proactive, intelligent, and automated. Advancements in artificial intelligence, behavioral analytics, automation, and cloud security integration are reshaping how organizations detect and respond to threats. By leveraging AI-driven threat intelligence, predictive analytics, and deception techniques, SIEM solutions will empower security teams to stay ahead of cyber adversaries. The future of threat hunting with SIEM is moving towards real-time, continuous, and predictive security monitoring, enabling organizations to detect and neutralize threats before they cause significant harm.

Final Thoughts: The Road Ahead for SIEM

Security Information and Event Management (SIEM) has undergone a remarkable transformation since its inception, evolving from a log management tool into a critical component of modern cybersecurity strategies. As cyber threats continue to grow in complexity and scale, SIEM must adapt to meet the demands of an increasingly connected and digitized world. Organizations rely on SIEM not only for security monitoring but also for compliance management, incident response, and advanced threat detection. The road ahead for SIEM is shaped by emerging technologies, evolving attack landscapes, and the need for greater efficiency in security operations. As SIEM solutions continue to evolve, organizations must prepare for a future where automation, artificial intelligence, cloud-native security, and extended detection capabilities redefine the role of SIEM in cybersecurity.

The integration of artificial intelligence and machine learning is one of the most significant advancements shaping the future of SIEM. Traditional SIEM solutions relied on predefined rules and correlation logic to detect security threats, but these approaches are becoming insufficient against sophisticated attacks that evolve in real time. AI-powered SIEM systems analyze vast amounts of security data, identify patterns, and adapt to emerging threats without requiring manual rule adjustments. Machine learning models enhance SIEM's ability to detect anomalies, distinguish between false positives and genuine threats, and improve overall detection accuracy. The adoption of AI-driven threat intelligence and predictive analytics will allow SIEM platforms to anticipate attacks before they occur, enabling security teams to take preemptive actions.

Cloud adoption continues to reshape SIEM architecture, driving the shift from traditional on-premises deployments to cloud-native security models. As organizations migrate workloads to cloud environments, SIEM solutions must provide seamless integration with cloud platforms such as Amazon Web Services (AWS), Microsoft Azure, and Google Cloud Platform (GCP). Cloud-native SIEM solutions offer greater scalability, faster deployment times, and automated security monitoring for cloud-based assets. The ability to ingest and analyze cloud logs, monitor API activity, and detect misconfigurations in real time ensures that SIEM remains relevant in modern hybrid and multi-cloud environments. The transition to cloud-based SIEM also enables organizations to reduce infrastructure costs and focus on security operations without the burden of managing on-premises hardware.

Automation and orchestration are redefining how organizations use SIEM to streamline security operations. Security Orchestration, Automation, and Response (SOAR) platforms are increasingly integrated with SIEM, allowing organizations to automate incident response workflows. The traditional challenge of SIEM has been the high volume of alerts, many of which require manual investigation by security analysts. Automation reduces response times by executing predefined remediation actions such as blocking malicious IP addresses, isolating compromised devices, or enforcing access control policies. By leveraging automated threat containment mechanisms, SIEM solutions can improve efficiency and reduce the workload on security teams, allowing them to focus on more complex security threats.

The evolution of SIEM also includes a stronger emphasis on user behavior analytics and identity-based security monitoring. Traditional SIEM systems primarily focused on network traffic, firewall activity, and endpoint security logs. However, the rise of Zero Trust security models has placed identity at the center of cybersecurity strategies. User and Entity Behavior Analytics (UEBA) enhances SIEM capabilities by continuously monitoring user actions, access requests, and privilege escalations. SIEM solutions must evolve to incorporate identity intelligence, enabling organizations to detect insider threats, compromised accounts, and unauthorized access attempts. The convergence of SIEM and identity-based security monitoring strengthens threat detection by providing contextual awareness of user behavior across enterprise systems.

Extended detection and response (XDR) is another innovation influencing the future of SIEM. Traditional SIEM solutions primarily relied on log aggregation and event correlation to detect threats. XDR extends this approach by integrating endpoint telemetry, network security analytics, cloud security monitoring, and identity-based threat detection into a unified platform. The fusion of SIEM and XDR capabilities provides a more comprehensive view of security incidents, allowing organizations to detect threats across multiple attack vectors. By combining SIEM's data collection capabilities with XDR's real-time threat analytics, security teams can achieve greater visibility and faster threat resolution. The growing adoption of XDR-driven SIEM will enhance cybersecurity resilience and improve response capabilities in an increasingly complex threat landscape.

The role of SIEM in compliance management will continue to expand as regulatory requirements become more stringent. Organizations across industries must comply with data protection regulations such as GDPR, HIPAA, PCI DSS, and ISO 27001. SIEM solutions simplify compliance by automating log collection, generating audit-ready reports, and enforcing security policies that align with regulatory frameworks. Future SIEM platforms will leverage AI-driven compliance automation, reducing the burden on security teams by continuously monitoring adherence to industry regulations. The ability to provide real-time compliance visibility will become a key differentiator for SIEM vendors as organizations seek to improve audit readiness and avoid regulatory penalties.

Threat intelligence integration will play a critical role in the evolution of SIEM, enabling organizations to stay ahead of emerging cyber threats. Future SIEM solutions will incorporate real-time threat intelligence feeds from global security research organizations, government agencies, and commercial threat intelligence providers. By correlating internal security events with external threat intelligence, SIEM platforms will provide deeper insights into evolving attack techniques and indicators of compromise. AI-driven threat intelligence analysis will enable SIEM to dynamically adjust detection rules based on newly discovered threats, improving its ability to detect sophisticated cyberattacks in real time.

The convergence of SIEM with proactive threat-hunting capabilities will redefine how organizations detect and mitigate security threats. Traditional SIEM systems primarily focused on reactive security measures, detecting threats based on predefined correlation rules. The future of SIEM involves proactive threat hunting, where security teams actively search for hidden threats within enterprise environments. AI-powered threat-hunting tools will enhance SIEM by providing analysts with advanced search capabilities, behavioral anomaly detection, and automated threat investigation workflows. Organizations that integrate proactive threat hunting with SIEM will gain a strategic advantage in identifying and neutralizing cyber threats before they escalate into major security incidents.

The road ahead for SIEM is defined by innovation, adaptability, and the need for continuous security improvements. The integration of artificial intelligence, cloud-native architectures, automation, and extended detection capabilities will transform SIEM into a more intelligent and efficient security platform. Organizations must embrace these advancements to enhance threat detection, streamline security operations, and strengthen their overall cybersecurity posture. As cyber threats continue to evolve, SIEM will remain a cornerstone of modern security operations, providing the visibility, automation, and intelligence needed to protect digital assets in an ever-changing threat landscape. The future of SIEM lies in its ability to evolve alongside emerging security challenges, ensuring that organizations can detect, respond to, and mitigate threats with greater speed and precision.

www.ingramcontent.com/pod-product-compliance
Lightning Source LLC
LaVergne TN
LVHW022314060326
832902LV00020B/3467